Stillness in Motion: Heart-Centered Meridian Practice

Modern Zen for All

Donald Hwong

Contents

Do not be troubled by the noise from your
head.
Trust your heart—it knows the way.
It carries you inward,
to a universe alive with love, peace, joy, and
vitality.
When your heart radiates its quiet light,
the mind becomes calm.
And in that universe,
you discover contentment,
and awakening.

Chapter Two

Preface

I've lived long enough to know: wisdom arises naturally at its own pace.

My life has crossed many borders — across places, cultures, professions, and inner worlds.

I was born in Shanghai, raised in Taiwan, educated in Japan, and spent decades in the United States, immersed in the high-tech boom. I witnessed the incredible rise of human ingenuity, from the days of telexing paper tapes, magnetic-core memories, and diode matrix for bootstrap, to today's world of artificial intelligence.

But alongside that outer journey, a quieter, deeper journey was unfolding.

My grandmother prayed to many gods; My father is a baptized three-generation Christian; I attended a Catholic high school in Japan; in university, I wandered through

Walden, Nietzsche, and Sartre, wrestling with life's big questions. At age 50, I turned inward, returning to my Chinese roots. Many teachers found me. Master Wu-Jue Miao-Tian introduced me to the practice of Chinese Zen. Master Hong-Chi Xiao taught me the healing art of Paida Lajin. Dr. John Young introduced the teaching of "Neti Neti" and "one consciousness". Yeh Tzu guided me into the flowing energetic practice of Motion Zen.

I practiced, I stumbled, I witnessed. I taught. I lived it, not just studied it.

Some of the most profound lessons came not from formal teachings, but from life itself:

- *Over five years in practicing the art of "fulfillment", I discovered the weight of my ego, simply by choosing to fulfill every request my wife made — even when it meant missing the final minutes of a basketball game or pausing at the climax of a favorite show. I realized how tightly I clung to small attachments and how liberating it was to let them go. Since there is always "yes" from me. My wife and I merged into one person - her.*

- *One day in a Hong Kong seafood restaurant, I*

pointed at a lively fish in the tank, and the moment it was carried away to be cooked, a piercing headache struck me — as if some invisible thread of life between us had snapped. It happened again and again, teaching me a humbling lesson about spiritual connection and the living web we are all part of.

- *And then, in January 2008, during a class in Los Angeles, I was struck by a simple but shattering realization: "Ah, I understand" is only for the mind. True spirituality needs no understanding — it surfaces from our heart.*

Now, at eighty, I am blessed with a healthy body, a peaceful heart, and a joyful life — not because I became anyone remarkable, but because I discovered something universal: **how to live like a child again.**

This book is not a record of achievements or credentials. It is a humble offering — a collection of personal realizations and lived experiences.

I sincerely hope that what you find here helps you rise above the noise and confusion of the world, and become aware of a broader, more spacious universe — one where all perspectives are welcomed, and none need to be clung to as your own.

May it help you trust the natural unfolding of life, with its own pace, its own rhythm. May it give you the energy to live with hope, curiosity, creativity, and a sense of discovery. And most of all, may it give you the courage to liberate yourself from any and all forms of bondage — to live lightly, joyfully, and fearlessly.

Chapter Three

End of A Digital Pilgrimage

"Civilization is but a physical manifestation of life. Our spirituality is always the same."

— Goethe

The Early Sparks

In 1967, I found myself immersed in a subject that didn't yet exist in books—**digital electronics**. I was studying at the University of California, Berkeley, where everything was new, raw, and experimental. There were no textbooks—only a scattering of research papers penned by pioneering professors. Our "toys" were digital flip-flops—basic logic gates that toggled between zero and one. That was the language of the future, though at the time, few could imagine it.

We didn't yet know we were lighting a spark that would grow into a digital wildfire.

Building the First Multi-User Computer

After graduation, I was fortunate to join a DARPA-funded project. Our mission: design the world's fastest multi-user computer capable of serving 50 simultaneous users. It sounded audacious in those days.

The architecture was built around a **12-inch by 20-inch cage**, each slot holding a printed circuit board. We designed with an 8-bit processor with **diode-matrix logic** to boot the system, and **magnetic core memory**—those tiny rings strung together like beads—to retain data.

We christened our creation *the microprocessor*. The term stuck—and not long after, **Intel adopted it**, launching their 4-bit and later 8-bit microprocessors, forever changing the world.

I witnessed the moment when engineering theory became real-world revolution.

From Hardware to Software—and Knowing When to Stop

In time, I found a software company. A Japanese conglomerate funded our vision, and I ran the company for ten years. Eventually, I sold it to a NASDAQ-listed firm. Not for money. Not because we failed.

I sold it because I realized something rare in tech: **there's only so much help people actually need**.

We had run out of meaningful ideas. Our engineers were busy inventing new features, but our users had long stopped asking for more. Like Microsoft Word—how many of its hundreds of functions do most people use?

At some point, I felt like I was polishing a hammer that no longer needed refining.

So I let it go.

A Quiet Realization

After years in the digital world, one truth emerged clearly:

Engineers are just bigger boys with bigger toys—for a supposedly better reason.

Some of our creations serve no real human need. Some merely enhance our laziness. The washing machine helped us avoid scrubbing clothes by hand. Was that innovation or indulgence? Even AI can make us mentally dependent on it.

Technology is not inherently good or bad. But **progress without purpose is hollow**.

Goethe's words echoed in my mind: *Civilization is but a physical manifestation of life*. It may evolve, accelerate, and adorn itself in circuit boards and silicon. But **our inner lives—our spiritual thread—remain unchanged**. Through centuries and empires, in palaces or pixels, the human heart still longs for meaning.

Return to Stillness

At the age of 50, I encountered a Chinese Zen master. Or perhaps he encountered me. Either way, the path was clear. I had surfed the waves of logic, data, and code long enough.

It was time to find the truth.

While the world chased faster processors and smarter machines, I began to follow something subtler—**a path**

that led not forward, but inward. A path beyond pro-ductivity. Beyond features. Beyond function.

Because in the end, no matter how sophisticated the tool or the toy, what we truly seek is not in the technology.

Chapter Four

Introduction

Not long ago, my son brought my four-year-old grandson, Josh, from Seattle to visit me. Josh is like a pinball in a pinball machine—constantly in motion, bouncing from one spot to another with unstoppable energy. As long as he's awake, he welcomes everything life throws his way—with a smile. A new toy, a new game, a stranger, or even a request—he accepts them all without hesitation, without resistance.

He doesn't cling, and he doesn't judge. He doesn't ask, "Do I like this?" or "Should I do that?" He simply lives. He may not stay with one thing for long, but he never holds on to anything. He moves on, light-hearted and curious, full of joy and presence.

Watching him, I found myself deeply moved. His uninhibited love for life stirred something inside me. A quiet question arose:

When was the last time I lived like that?

When was the last time I hopped instead of walked, laughed without a reason, accepted each moment without needing it to be different?

Why can't we all live like that? Why not embrace life as it comes, without overthinking, without judgment? Some may say, "But won't people think we're being childish or naïve?" But do you think Josh worries about how he's perceived? Is he concerned about awakening, about healing his past, or achieving enlightenment?

Of course not. Josh lives in the now—completely. He doesn't analyze or label his experience. He is simply **alive**, fully and joyfully.

This book is born from that moment of reflection. It is about returning to that childlike wholeness—not childishness, but the original purity of heart that spiritual traditions across the world point us back to.

Drawing from the teachings of Jesus, the wisdom of the Buddha, the ancient insights of Traditional Chinese Medicine (TCM), and modern scientific understanding, this book seeks to illuminate the *missing ingredients* that allow us to truly love life again.

It offers not just philosophy, but practical ways to restore vitality and simplicity, so that joy rises naturally from within.

You'll learn how to direct your awareness inward, allowing you to feel your life energy—Qi—moving and pulsing inside you.

This energy, once felt, is unmistakable. It brings joy, satisfaction, liveliness, and a sense of unexplainable contentment. It reminds you that you are not separate from nature or from the sacred—you are its expression.

Through body-based practices, focused mind, and a sense of play, this book invites you to explore a path that is deeply spiritual *and* profoundly energizing. You'll meet ideas that are ancient, yet presented in simple language. No jargon. No dogma. Just guidance to help you remember what you already know: that life is to be lived fully, not figured out.

This book flows in four parts—like the rhythm of life itself.

We begin with **The Inquiry**, where questions arise and old truths are re-examined. Then comes **The Zen Lin-**

eage, a return to the roots of Zen and its teachings. Then **The Heart Zen Practice**, introducing you a breathing technique, witnessing internal Qi and the gateway practice of "The Three Center Alignment". Last is **Everybody @ Each Moment.**

You don't need to remember these parts. Just walk with me. The path will unfold.

Because many of the original teachings shared in these pages were developed in Chinese, translating them into English has been a heartfelt journey. While today's technology helps with editing, please forgive any imperfections. The intention is sincere. The spirit behind every sentence is shared with love.

And yes, this will be a *fun* book to read. Not heavy or solemn. A book of lightness. A book of breath. A book for those who want to reclaim their childlike vitality, spiritual joy, and the ability to hop—yes, hop—through life again.

Part I: The Inquiry

"Not all those who wander are lost." — J.R.R. Tolkien

Chapter Six

The Courage to Enjoy Life

As we grow up, we are taught to be responsible. We are taught what is right and what is wrong. These lessons, drilled into us by parents, teachers, and society, shape our internal compass. Over time, they evolve into the guiding principles of our lives.

At first, they serve us well—giving structure, offering direction, building character. But slowly, imperceptibly, these principles begin to solidify into rules that bind us. Responsibility morphs into obligation. Morality becomes a script. And our lives are no longer freely chosen, but carefully measured—governed by what others expect of us.

We build our identities on these foundations: good child, reliable adult, dutiful partner, loyal employee. We strive to meet the standards laid out for us by tradition, by culture, by family. And in doing so, we often forget to ask ourselves: *Is this the life I truly want?*

Changing course feels daunting. Even the mere thought of it stirs anxiety. To deviate from the expected path requires more than desire—it requires courage. Because to voice a new idea, to chase a different dream, to say *no* to what has always been accepted—this can feel like rebellion. It can feel like letting people down. And perhaps most difficult of all, it can feel like letting yourself down if things don't work out.

This is why so many of us remain stuck. Without first trying, we cannot develop confidence. And without confidence, we cannot find the courage to begin. Fear—fear of failure, fear of judgment, fear of regret—overtakes us. So we stay quiet. We stay the same. And life, rich with possibilities, quietly passes us by.

But joy does not grow from safety. Fulfillment does not bloom from conformity. If we truly want to enjoy life, we must be willing to live it. And to live fully means to risk, to explore, to play, to change, to discover.

To enjoy life takes courage.

The courage to say, *I want something more.*

The courage to admit, *I don't have all the answers, but I'm willing to search.*

The courage to live by your own rhythm, even when it's different from everyone else's.

And here's the truth: You don't have to abandon responsibility to embrace joy. You don't have to reject love to follow your heart. You simply need to follow your heart and not your over-thinking mind. Just be nakedly honest about your true feelings. Laugh and cry at will, with courage.

You will discover in later chapters what the true meaning of life is—and how to genuinely enjoy the **flow** of life. Not by resisting, planning, or worrying—but by learning how to tune into your own energy, your own nature, your own spontaneous spirit. The answers are not out there—they are already within you, waiting to be uncovered.

So if there's a whisper in your heart calling for a new beginning, let it speak. If you feel an inner nudge toward something unknown, let it guide you. That's not recklessness. That's life asking you to participate—fully, joyfully, courageously.

May the courage be with us all.

The courage to feel. The courage to trust.

The courage to enjoy this beautiful, unrepeatable life.

Chapter Seven

Fragmented Learning of Nature

The Original Teacher

Nature is the original teacher—quiet, patient, and infinitely wise.

In nature, everything exists in harmony. Trees, rivers, insects, birds, soil, and sunlight all depend on each other. They interact, influence, and support one another in a vast, self-sustaining web of life. Nothing survives on its own. Anything that detaches from this living network eventually withers away. This is the essence of wholeness.

Nature Is Never in a Hurry

There's another profound lesson nature teaches: **you cannot rush it**.

A flower blooms only when it is ready. You cannot force it open. An apple ripens in its own time. Spring arrives exactly when it should—and never earlier. Summer does not come because we demand it. Everything in nature follows a natural rhythm and perfect timing. No force, no stress—just flow.

But we humans, in our attempt to understand nature, took a different path.

We analyze. We categorize. We break things down into parts so we can label and measure them. While this approach gives us some knowledge, it also creates distance from the whole. What once was a unified system becomes fragmented.

The Problem with Fragmentation

Our modern way of life reflects a deep disconnect from the natural flow of wholeness. In nearly every domain of human endeavor, we have replaced the organic with the mechanical, the integrated with the divided. This fragmentation, though well-intended, often leads to confusion, inefficiency, and suffering.

Let's explore how this plays out:

Medicine: Treating the Parts, Losing the Person

In most modern healthcare systems, the human body is treated like a machine made of separate parts. Specialists focus on organs in isolation: a cardiologist treats the heart, a neurologist the brain, a gastroenterologist the digestive system. But no organ exists independently. The heart affects the brain, the gut influences emotion, and the lungs respond to grief.

This compartmentalization can lead to incomplete healing. One symptom is treated while its root cause, often located elsewhere in the body—or in the mind or emotional state—is ignored. Patients end up with multiple prescriptions, each addressing a part, while the whole person is overlooked.

The ancient systems of medicine—like Traditional Chinese Medicine or Ayurveda—treat the person as an ecosystem. Modern medicine is beginning to rediscover this approach, but the dominant model still leans toward division rather than integration.

Education: Learning Without Connection

From early schooling onward, children are taught in separated subjects: math, language, science, history, art. Each discipline is treated as a stand-alone silo. Rarely are students shown how these areas connect—how music relates to math, how science is rooted in philosophy, or how history shapes the present.

This fragmented approach produces knowledge without wisdom. Students may memorize facts, but struggle to see patterns, make connections, or understand how their learning applies to real life. Worse, many grow up believing they are "bad at math" or "not artistic" because of how segmented their education was, rather than being shown how all knowledge flows as one.

An integrated education would teach students to see life as a whole, to cultivate curiosity across boundaries, and to apply learning creatively to the world around them.

Spirituality: Dividing the Indivisible

Even the realm of spirituality has not escaped compartmentalization. We often see teachings that focus only on the **body** (through postures, breathing, or diet), or exclusively on the **mind** (through meditation, concentration, or affirmations), or solely on the **spirit** (through devotion, transcendence, or metaphysical understanding).

But these aspects of ourselves are not separate. The body affects the mind. The mind shapes the spirit. The spirit informs the body. They are three expressions of one life force.

When we neglect the integration of these three, we can become imbalanced. A person focused solely on mental clarity may neglect the body's wisdom. Someone absorbed in spiritual experiences might forget to tend to their physical health or emotional well-being. Others may become trapped in physical performance, never touching the inner stillness of their being.

True spiritual practice honors the whole. It cultivates vitality in the body, clarity in the mind, and openness in the heart—all at once.

The Invitation to Wholeness

This book offers a quiet but powerful invitation: **return to wholeness.**

We will explore a few simple yet profound practices—drawn from ancient wisdom and personal experience—that can help you reconnect your **body**, **mind**, and **spirit** into one integrated flow.

When these three aspects are aligned, they support each other like roots, trunk, and leaves of the same tree. Life becomes smoother, more natural. You begin to live not against nature, but in rhythm with it.

This is not a path of effort, control, or willpower. It is a return to something you've always had: the natural intelligence of life itself.

When you begin to live from this place of integration, something beautiful happens:

You realize you are not separate from nature. You are nature.

And nature, when whole, always finds its way.

Chapter Eight

The Tree of Knowledge and the Illusion of Knowing

I sometimes envy the era when **Leonardo da Vinci** lived.

Back then, the **tree of knowledge** was still small. Its roots, trunk, and branches were visible to the curious eye. A single human mind—driven by curiosity and wonder—could travel freely from art to anatomy, from mechanics to movement, and from observation to inspiration. **Everything was connected.**

Da Vinci painted the human form not just with color, but with **understanding**—his knowledge of anatomy deepened his art. He studied birds and invented flying machines. The body's movement translated into the gears of mechanical design. Nothing was out of reach, because it all felt like **one harmonious whole**.

In contrast, today's tree of knowledge has grown vast and fragmented. It stretches into the sky with millions of branches and uncountable leaves. To even touch one branch in a lifetime is rare. Most of us spend our lives studying just **one leaf**, often mistaking it for the entire tree.

Fragmentation: Mistaking the Leaf for the Tree

The problem is not that we learn too little—but that we **fail to see the whole**.

Modern knowledge has been dissected and divided into countless fields: medicine, physics, art, psychology, philosophy, theology, data science, and more. Each has its own language, rules, and tribes. Each guards its domain, often with pride. But life itself is **not compartmentalized**.

Nature does not divide the universe into subjects. It **flows**—with every part affecting every other. But in our modern age, we study fragments and forget their relationships. We mistake the **part for the whole**, the **leaf for the tree**.

Worse, we become **confident in our conclusions**, even as we stand on limited ground. As if examining a single thread gives us authority over the entire tapestry.

What Does "Knowledge" Really Mean?

In Chinese, the word for "knowledge" is formed by two characters:

- **(xué)** – to learn

- **(wèn)** – to ask

Nowhere does it imply that we "know." True knowledge, in its original spirit, is not something we possess. It is an **ongoing process**—a dance of questioning, exploring, and humbling ourselves before the unknown.

The **Buddhist tradition** sharpens this point even further:

"Ignorance is not the absence of knowledge. Ignorance is thinking you already know."

This mistaken certainty—that we know enough to judge the whole tree—is what keeps us blind. We make decisions, form judgments, and live rigidly based on a few pieces of information. We treat our fragment as the whole truth.

But a **leaf is not a branch**.

A **branch is not the trunk**.

And the **trunk is not the root**.

From Leaf to Root: Returning to Wholeness

To regain harmony in our understanding, we must **reverse our path**:

- From the **leaf**, we trace back to the **branch**

- From the **branch**, we return to the **trunk**

- And from the **trunk**, we seek the **root**

And what is the root of all knowledge?

It is not written in books or stored in data.

The **root is the universal consciousness**—the intelligence that gives rise to all things. It animates the tree, the earth, the human being, the question, and the answer. It is not something we *know* intellectually—it is something we **tap into** intuitively.

We can't acquire the whole tree of knowledge in one lifetime. But we can stay rooted. We can trust that if we connect to the root, we are in touch with **life itself**.

Trust the Tree. Trust the Universe.

We often overestimate our ability to change the world and underestimate the wisdom of the world itself.

The **universe** does not make mistakes.

Nature does not rush.

Everything has its **own rhythm and timing**—from the blossoming of a flower to the ripening of insight.

As human beings, we have limited power to control or redesign these natural patterns. But we have infinite power to **trust**, to **observe**, and to **align ourselves** with the rhythm of life.

Let go of the need to master every branch.

Instead, stay close to the **root**. Let it nourish you.

From Knowledge to Wisdom

The goal of learning is not to accumulate facts—it is to awaken to **interconnectedness**.

Da Vinci once lived in a world where the branches were still close, and the connections visible. We live in a world where specialization has made the whole almost invisible. But the path back to wholeness still exists.

It lies in **humility**, in the willingness to ask, to learn, to wonder—without clinging to the illusion that we already know.

Because once we truly see the tree,

we stop trying to own it—

and instead, bow in reverence before it.

Chapter Nine

What I learned from Josh

I n my classes, I often share a simple but profound teaching from the Bible. In *Matthew 18:3*, Jesus said,

> *"Truly I tell you, unless you change and become like little children, you will never enter the kingdom of heaven."*

Many spiritual interpretations of this verse emphasize the cultivation of innocence, humility, and mental stillness. But I believe Jesus was pointing to something far more complete — not just a mindset, but a **whole-being return** to the childlike state — one that includes the body, the energy, the spirit, and above all, the **unshakable love of life**.

What amazes me most about Josh is how he lives beyond time, beyond schedules, plans, and all the man-made rules and regulations we adults cling to. He is not governed by a calendar or a to-do list. He lives by something far more ancient and true: the rhythm of his own being as guided by nature.

Josh moves through life with his body, mind, and spirit integrated into one seamless wholeness. There's no inner conflict, no compartmentalization—just one unified expression of life in motion. He is driven by energy—by a life force that flows through him like a current of vitality. When this life force is full and radiant, he lights up the world around him. He springs into the day with open arms, a bright smile, and a heart brimming with joy and love. He welcomes every gift nature throws at him—curious, unafraid, and fully present. He has no preference or judgment.

But when that energy is depleted, he doesn't fight it. He doesn't push through or pretend. He simply stops. The whole system shuts down—body, mind, and heart. The body goes to rest, and the heart takes a pause from feeling. And just like that, he surrenders into stillness, without resistance or guilt.

This, I've come to realize, is not childish—it's wisdom in its purest form.

To live life to its fullest, we don't need more effort, more planning, or more control. We need to observe what Josh is going through. And then—humble ourselves enough to copy that model. Live when the life force flows. Rest when it doesn't. Act with joy, receive with love, and surrender without fear. It's that simple.

The Whole Child: More Than Just a Mind-set

Too many spiritual teachings fixate only on the mind: calm your thoughts, detach from the world, transcend the ego. While those may be helpful practices, they often miss what makes a child truly divine — the **integrated aliveness** of their entire being.

A child is:

- Physically **fluid and vibrant**, full of spontaneous movement.

- Energetically **unblocked**, their life force flows without stagnation.

- Emotionally **free**, able to feel and release without clinging.

- Spiritually **open**, connected to wonder, mystery, and presence.

- Mentally **positive**, always looking at life through the lens of possibility.

- And most of all — driven by the **love of life**.

Children do not try to achieve peace. They **live** it through their direct and open-hearted engagement with the universe.

Heaven Is Not Escape — It's a Return to Joy

Heaven, then, is not a destination beyond this world. It is a state of being in **full harmony** with life — body, mind, and spirit dancing together, without conflict. A child doesn't need convincing to be joyful. Joy is their default. Why? Because they trust life. They greet it with a smile, with movement, with curiosity. They **love** it.

As adults, we often lose this love. We replace it with fear, resistance, overthinking, and control. We stop playing. We stiffen. We judge ourselves. We forget the natural rhythm of delight that once pulsed through us.

But the good news is: it's not lost forever. It's just buried. And with intention, we can **return** to it.

The Path Is Not Upward — It's Inward and Backward

To become a child again is not to regress or pretend. It is to **reconnect** — to walk back into the garden of your original being, where everything was alive and welcomed. That includes:

- **Breathing with openness**, like a baby who hasn't yet learned tension.

- **Moving with lightness**, free of rigidity or self-consciousness.

- **Feeling fully**, without shame or suppression.

- **Laughing easily**, even after pain.

- **Trusting the flow**, not controlling the outcome.

- **Loving life**, simply because it's there.

This love of life isn't about denying difficulties. Children feel pain deeply — but they don't hold onto it. They don't identify with their wounds. Their default attitude is **hopeful**. This is their superpower — and it's the very spirit of heaven.

Living Joyfully Is the Greatest Spiritual Practice

I often say:

"you don't need to meditate for hours to find God."

Sometimes, what you need is to **run barefoot on grass**, feel the sun on your skin, giggle at something silly, or stare wide-eyed at a butterfly. That childlike delight is not a distraction from the spiritual path — it *is* the path.

And it is powered by one thing: your **love of life**.

This love makes your cells healthier. It improves your posture, your breath, your digestion, your sleep. It opens your heart. It heals your trauma. It transforms your relationships. And it aligns your consciousness with something far greater than your ego — with the **universal joy** of being.

To Enter Heaven Is to Say Yes to Life

So when Jesus said, *"Unless you become like little children..."* he wasn't just talking about purity. He was speaking of that **unified state of being** where body, mind, and spirit rejoice in each other's presence. Where every part of you says **yes** to life.

That yes is what opens the gates.

Chapter Ten

Detach from the Physical Reality

We often hear spiritual teachings speak of detachment - letting go of painful memories, harmful relationships, or even joyful attachments. Yet true detachment runs far deeper than this surface-level understanding. The *Diamond Sutra*, a cornerstone of Mahayana Buddhism, challenges us to detach not just from worldly suffering but from all conceptual frameworks, declaring:

> *"Dharma is not Dharma; that is why it is called Dharma."*

This paradoxical statement reveals that even our most cherished spiritual teachings must ultimately be released.

This radical approach finds parallel expressions across wisdom traditions. Advaita Vedanta's **"Neti Neti" (Not**

this, not this) systematically negates all identifications - body, mind, experiences, even spiritual realizations. Zen Buddhism's **"Beginner's Mind" (Shoshin)**, as taught by Master Shunryu Suzuki, similarly invites us to meet each moment fresh, unburdened by accumulated knowledge:

> *"In the beginner's mind there are many possibilities; in the expert's mind there are few."*

The Double-Edged Sword of Spiritual Knowledge

Most seekers begin their journey by accumulating spiritual knowledge - sacred texts, guru teachings, and meditation techniques. Yet this very accumulation can become the new obstacle. Like trying to see the moon while focusing on the finger pointing at it, we mistake spiritual concepts for the truth they attempt to describe.

The *Mandukya Upanishad* warns:

> *"The Self is beyond all concepts, beyond words, beyond thought."*

When we cling to teachings about enlightenment, we create a new form of bondage. Even the most profound philosophy becomes another layer of the mind's illusion when held as absolute truth.

Neti Neti: The Alchemy of Negation

The ancient practice of *Neti Neti* offers a powerful methodology for this radical detachment. Unlike positive spiritual practices that seek to acquire or achieve something, this is a path of systematic negation:

- Is the Self the body? *Neti* (Not this)

- Is it thoughts or emotions? *Neti*

- Is it spiritual experiences? *Neti*

- Is it even the concept of enlightenment? *Neti*

This relentless negation burns away all false identifications until only the indescribable reality remains. As the great sage Nisargadatta Maharaj would say:

"When all false identifications are dropped, what remains is your true nature."

Beginner's Mind: The Zen of Unknowing

Zen practice brings this same insight through different means. The Beginner's Mind isn't just for novices - it's the essential attitude for even the most advanced practitioners. It represents:

1. **Freedom from expertise** - The more we think we know, the less we actually see

2. **Immediate presence** - Meeting each moment without the filter of past experience

3. **Creative not-knowing** - The fertile ground where true insight emerges

As one Zen koan challenges:

"If you meet the Buddha, kill the Buddha."

This shocking statement reminds us that even our highest spiritual concepts must be surrendered.

The Final Detachment: From Seeking Itself

Here we encounter the great paradox: the seeker must ultimately detach from seeking itself. All spiritual paths are like rafts — essential for crossing the river, but burdensome if carried afterward. The moment we believe we're making "spiritual progress," we've created another illusion.

I remember vividly, in January 2008, during an annual gathering in Los Angeles, I was sitting quietly when a sudden realization struck me — so simple and yet so undeniable:

The notion of "Ah, I understand" is for the mind only. It got nothing to do with our spirit.

We don't need to understand. Spirituality, awakening, truth — these live beyond understanding. They unfold naturally, effortlessly, and no grasping of the mind is required.

This insight dissolved years of accumulated striving. It reminded me that the most profound truths are not principles we acquire but spaces we open into — when we relax our grip on the mind's endless seeking.

The *Bhagavad Gita* describes this as *"Stithaprajna"* — remaining undisturbed amidst all experiences. In Christian mysticism, Meister Eckhart speaks of *"gelassenheit"* — letting go of even the concept of God. These all point to the same truth: complete surrender of all mental constructs.

The Freedom of No-Position

True spirituality isn't about reaching some exalted state, but about the radical freedom of having no position to defend, no identity to maintain, no teaching to cling to, no detachment to be detached.

In the end, we discover that what we've been seeking was never lost - it was only obscured by our very attempts to find it. This is the ultimate joke of enlightenment - that we realize there was never anything to attain in the first place.

The Necessity of Detachment

The practice of detachment only becomes necessary when you believe what you see, hear, touch, and experience through your senses is *real*—that it has substance, permanence, and independent existence.

If this physical world—this house of noise and sensation—is believed to be the ultimate reality, then detachment is your medicine. It becomes a tool to help you loosen your grip on illusions that otherwise entangle the mind and trap the spirit. You practice letting go because you are caught. You are caught because you believe.

But the very question—*Is it real?*—deserves deeper reflection. That question will be explored more fully in the next chapter. For now, consider this: What if what you see is no more real than a mirage shimmering on a desert road? What if what you hear is but an echo in a canyon of dreams?

If you begin to perceive this world not as solid truth, but as a temporary projection, a momentary display, then your relationship to it changes completely.

In Buddhist tradition, this dimension of impermanence and illusion is called the **Saha world**—the world of endurance, where beings suffer, strive, and cling, thinking all of it is real. But when you see the Saha world as it is—a fleeting illusion—you stop reacting, striving, and grasping. You stop needing to detach, because you were never truly attached to begin with. The hooks fall away on their own.

At that moment, the **spiritual world**, which was never absent, begins to surface. Not in a faraway heaven, but here. Right here, beneath and behind the veil of illusion.

The spiritual world was always present, quietly waiting. It is the reality behind the reflection. It is clarity behind confusion, stillness behind chaos, truth behind appearances.

In other words, once you see the physical world for what it is—a layered illusion—you don't need to escape it. You've already transcended it. **You've turned the Saha world into a garden of flowers rather than a prison.**

And with that shift, detachment disappears. You don't have detachment to practice. You simply awaken. As Josh would say:

"I don't need to understand. I just play and play!"

Chapter Eleven

Reality Is Not Emptiness

The Many Faces of Reality

What is reality?

It's one of the oldest, deepest, and most elusive questions human beings have ever asked. And every spiritual tradition offers its own lens.

In **Buddhism**, reality is described as **emptiness**—not a void, but a spaciousness in which all things arise and fall. "Form is emptiness, and emptiness is form," says the *Heart Sutra*, meaning that nothing exists independently or permanently. Everything is interdependent, always changing, and ultimately without a fixed identity.

In **Advaita Vedanta**, reality is called **One Conscious-ness**. Beneath all appearances—our bodies, minds, emotions—is a single, undivided awareness. "You are That," declare the ancient Upanishads. All is One, and the separation we perceive is illusion.

In **Christianity**, Jesus taught that **"The Kingdom of God is within you."** The divine realm is not outside us in space or time, but alive in the here and now, in the depths of our being.

These teachings may sound abstract or mystical, and indeed, they point to something that cannot be fully captured in words.

A Physical Perspective: Senses and Limitations

So let's take a more grounded view. Let's say—for now—that **reality is what we can see, hear, touch, smell, and taste**.

This seems obvious. The chair you sit on is real. The sound of a bird is real. The smell of rain, the warmth of sunlight—all feel real to us.

But how far can we really see?

How well can we really hear?

When a tsunami approaches, animals flee to high ground long before humans are aware. Birds take flight. Elephants move inland. They sense the shift, while we—creatures who pride ourselves on intelligence—often miss the signals.

Our **physical senses** are limited.

Even more, we each **interpret** what we sense differently.

Two people in the same room might hear the same sentence but walk away with different meanings. We each live in **our own version of partial reality**, shaped by our conditioning, memory, and emotion.

And what's more—**reality is never static**.

Trees grow and stretch toward the sun. Raindrops form puddles, puddles form streams, and streams become rivers that flow into oceans. A flower blooms in the morning and wilts by nightfall.

Only This Moment Is Real

There's a line I remember vividly from a Shakespearean movie—**The Taming of the Shrew**—featuring **Richard Burton and Elizabeth Taylor**.

Richard Burton, in a moment of powerful simplicity, says:

"Now I am here. The time that I was there is gone forever."

That line stuck with me for life.

It points to something many spiritual teachings agree on:

Only **this moment** is real.

But there's a paradox: the moment you notice the moment, it's already gone. The present is fluid, slipping away even as we try to hold it. So if the moment itself is ever-changing, what can we say is truly real?

The Flow of Tao

The answer that resonates most deeply with me comes from the ancient Chinese wisdom of **Taoism**.

The **Tao**, or "The Way", is not a thing. It's a living principle—the flow of life, the pulse of existence itself.

In the *Tao Te Ching*, Laozi writes:

"The Tao that can be spoken is not the eternal Tao."

In other words, if you can describe it, grasp it, or contain it—it's not it.

The Tao cannot be held still. You can't stop it, can't control it.

You can only **flow** with it.

This same truth is echoed in **Chan (Zen) Buddhism**, which shares deep roots with Taoism. There's a phrase from Chinese Chan teaching that encapsulates this paradox beautifully:

(Sui yuan bu bian, bu bian sui yuan)

This can be translated as:

"Flow with conditions without being changed; do not change, and yet adapt to conditions."

It means: stay grounded in your true nature (which is unchanging), and at the same time, flow with the changes of the world without resistance. Like water taking the shape of any container, yet always remaining water. Like the moon reflected in many rivers—ever-adapting, yet never losing its essence.

In other words, **reality is not about fixing or holding onto anything**. It is about maintaining inner stillness while dancing with outer change.

The Tao is this ungraspable dance. It flows, and you flow with it.

And if you try to stop it, define it, or control it—you miss it.

To live in harmony with the Tao is to live the wisdom of both **emptiness and form**, **movement and stillness**, **change and presence**.

Energy and Qi: The Invisible Real

So what is it that enables the flows?

It is **energy**. It is **Qi** (CH-E-E).

In modern science, the term **"energy"** first appeared in 1807, introduced by **Thomas Young**, a British polymath. He used it to describe a measurable force that animates movement and physical phenomena.

But long before that—**over 2,000 years ago**—the Chinese classics had already described **Qi (chi)**, the invisible life force that flows through all things. In the *Huangdi Neijing* (Yellow Emperor's Inner Classic), Qi is described not only as vital energy but also as the **fundamental fabric of reality**.

And as we know today from physics, **energy never dies**. It only **transforms**—from **kinetic (dynamic) energy** to **potential energy**, and back again. A rolling wave eventually becomes still water. A falling tree stores sunlight as growth, then returns it to the soil as nutrients. The energy remains, even if its form changes.

Qi behaves the same way. It shifts between movement and stillness, between expression and rest. You cannot see it or hold it—but you can feel its presence when you slow down, open your senses, and quiet your mind. We will discuss in more detail in later chapters.

Living the Reality of Flow

To live in alignment with the **Tao** is not to chase or grasp reality—it is to flow with it.

To become aware of **Qi** is not to define or capture it—it is to **attune** to it.

When we stop clinging to fixed ideas of reality, we begin to taste its true nature: **fluid, alive, interconnected, and mysterious**.

Have you ever tried to float down a river?

First of all, you must **relax**, fully. Only then can you **float**.

If you struggle, resist, or bring in any kind of intentional control, you sink.

Second, you must **follow the river's current**. If you try to move against it, to go your own way, you no longer float—you fight.

This is how life flows. The more we try to resist it or assert our fixed ideas, the more disconnected and exhausted we become.

But when we surrender to the movement, when we trust the natural current of Qi—we are carried effortlessly.

Yezi once advised, **"Life is like a bus. You don't know who's going to get on, or who's going to get off. It just is."**

That's the flow of Tao. People enter our lives, and they leave.

Opportunities arise, and they dissolve.

Joy visits, sorrow follows.

Nothing is permanent, nothing can be predicted.

Our task is not to control the passengers or steer the route.

It is to stay **present** on the ride, trusting the bus knows where it's going—even if we don't.

So what is reality?

Not what the eye sees, not what the ear hears, not what the mind believes.

Reality is **this moment in motion**.

Reality is **the Tao flowing through you**.

Reality is **the Qi pulsing in your breath, your cells, your awareness**.

You don't need to believe it.

You only need to feel it.

And when you do—you are no longer separate from life.

You are life itself.

Reality is not Emptiness - It Simply Is

Now that we recognize reality cannot be a fixed state—never constant, never permanent—we must accept that reality is only ever a **flow**.

Many philosophers, religious leaders, and spiritual teachers have described this fluid, impermanent nature of reality using terms like **emptiness**. While their insights point toward something important, I believe this tendency to label and conceptualize is itself a form of over-interpretation.

In my view, reality is just reality.

It is not a projection, not a symbol, not a teaching. It is what is, when it is. It arises. It changes. It disappears. It is born, it dies, and it exists—**only for a moment**. And then it flows on.

More importantly, **reality does not flow randomly**.

It flows in accordance with the **law of cause and effect**—what many call **karma**. Every moment is shaped by the moment before it. Every phenomenon sets the conditions for what comes next. This is not something we can control. No one escapes it. No teacher, no method, no belief can bypass the natural unfolding of karmic consequences. It is **beyond our personal will**.

What is truly *empty* is not the phenomenon itself—but **our recognition of it through the mind**. The moment we begin to process reality—analyze it, name it, compare it, prefer or reject it—we are no longer living in the experience itself. We are living in illusion.

All interpretation is illusion.

All judgment is illusion.

All knowledge, all labels, even spiritual teachings—if they exist only in the mind—are illusions of reality, not reality itself.

Reality cannot be captured.

It cannot be preserved.

It can only be experienced **by flowing with it**, not by trying to hold on.

So let's be clear: **Reality is not emptiness**—reality is. What's empty is our **mental grasping** at it.

What's real is what **cannot be grasped**, but only lived, fully, now—within the unfolding rhythm of cause and effect.

Chapter Twelve

Beyond Understanding: From Words to Spirit

1. The Birth of Imitation

It begins with a single word.

Mama. Papa.

From that moment, we are taught to imitate. To copy. To mirror what's in front of us. That's how the machinery of learning starts: observe, absorb, repeat.

Then comes curiosity. We ask:

"What is this?"

Followed by:

"How do I do that?"

And soon enough:

"I like this, I don't like that."

This is how we begin to build our internal library of knowledge—by naming, liking, disliking. It's a structure built entirely on imitation and classification.

2. The World Built on Words

What we call *understanding* is, in truth, a system of labels—words, images, ideas—all created by the human mind. These are not nature's tools. They are not universal. They are inventions.

And yet, we rely on them. In the physical world, we must.

We must distinguish:

- a red light from a green one,

- a one-dollar bill from a hundred-dollar bill,

- a firecracker from a gunshot.

To survive and navigate this society, knowing *what is* and *how to* is essential. No one questions that.

But...

3. The Limits of Knowing

When it comes to the spiritual world—a realm of love, peace, and transcendence—this system of knowing fails.

You cannot think your way to peace.

You cannot analyze your way to joy.

You cannot understand your way to love.

You may read a thousand scriptures, attend endless retreats, repeat the mantras perfectly—yet if you have not *experienced* stillness, it remains unknown.

Words can point to it.

Concepts can hint at it.

But none of them *are* it.

4. Experience Interrupted

Even when we attempt to experience love or stillness, the mind interferes.

The five senses keep delivering their reports:

"Look at this."

"Listen to that."

"This feels good."

"This smells bad."

"This tastes sweet."

The mind, ever the interpreter, adds commentary:

"This reminds me of..."

"This is just like last time..."

"I don't want this again..."

And so the moment is lost.

The joy is filtered.

The love is named.

The peace is judged.

What was direct becomes distant.

5. The Only Way In

So how do we experience the spiritual directly?

We must quiet the mind.

But here's the paradox:

The mind cannot quiet itself.

It is not designed for silence.

It is a receiver, constantly processing information from the five senses.

So we do not fight the mind.

We redirect it.

6. The Inner Flashlight

The mind is like a flashlight. Wherever it points, it lights up.

If it points outward—toward sound, sight, thought—it remains busy.

If it turns inward—toward breath, energy, presence—it begins to settle.

And this is the path:

- Don't try to stop the mind.

- Simply point it elsewhere.

7. Turning Inward

In my experience, the most natural and effective way is to refocus the mind on your internal life force **using your heart**:

- On the flow of *chi*,

- On the vibration of your *chakras*,

- On the quiet hum of *aliveness* within.

These are not fantasies. They are perceptible—once you learn to feel with your heart.

When the heart becomes aware of internal energy, the mind begins to rest.

Not in sleep, but in stillness.

Not in thought, but in presence.

And in that stillness, the heart takes over.

Not the love of a story.

Not the love of someone.

But love itself.

8. A Wordless Knowing

This love cannot be labeled.

This joy cannot be remembered.

This peace cannot be grasped.

It can only be *lived*.

And that, perhaps, is the greatest mystery of all:

> Every understanding is only a label.
>
> And spirituality cannot be labeled.
>
> It must be experienced—or not at all.

Practice: Refocus the Flashlight

Tonight before sleep, turn off all distractions.

Lie still.

Bring your attention not to your thoughts, but to the inside of your body.

Feel the rhythm of your breath.

Feel the warmth in your hands, your chest, your belly.

Sense the hum—the aliveness—without naming it.

Do not ask, *What is this?*

Simply feel with your heart.

That is enough.

Chapter Thirteen

What Is Awakening?

We use the word *awakening* often in spiritual or philosophical contexts, but what does it really mean?

To awaken, by definition, is to rise from sleep, to emerge from a dream. It is a shift—a radical transition from one state of consciousness to another. We move from being unaware to being aware. From being caught in illusions to perceiving something more real, more vast, more true.

But in our pursuit of *enlightenment*, a natural question arises:

Where are we awakening from? And what are we awakening into?

The Two States of Awakening

To understand awakening, we must understand both the unawakened and the awakened states.

The Unawakened State: The Busy Mind

In the unawakened state, we are fully immersed in the *noise of the mind*. Our awareness is entangled in thoughts, memories, projections, and judgments. We analyze, compare, label, discriminate, and assert. We carry knowledge and experience like badges of honor. We believe we are our opinions. We are convinced of our self-importance.

This is the state of the ego—the one who must be right, who must control, who must know. It is a constant loop of interpretation, fear, pride, and attachment.

And yet, we call this "normal." Most people spend their entire lives in this state.

The Awakened State: Direct Experience of Truth

When awakening happens, the grip of the mind loosens.

Instead of thinking about reality, we *see* reality. Directly. Without the interference of thought.

There's a profound stillness. A clarity that doesn't come from intellect but from *being*. In this state, we are no longer separate observers of the universe. We are the universe experiencing itself.

The awakened state is not about acquiring something new. It's about returning to what is already there—your original nature. That silent awareness beneath all thoughts. The timeless presence beyond birth and death.

Why the Mind Cannot Awaken

Here lies the paradox: The mind can seek, learn, study, debate, and quote—but it cannot awaken.

Why?

Because the mind is the dream. The awakening happens *from* the mind—not within it.

No teaching, no guru, no book, no analysis can force this shift. They can inspire it, point to it, but they are not *it*. As the **Diamond Sutra** says:

> "The true Dharma is no Dharma. The no-Dharma is the Dharma."

This cryptic line means: even the teachings themselves must be let go. They are tools, not truths. Maps, not destinations.

At best, teachings offer you *pointers*. But awakening is a direct experience—personal, internal, and irreversible.

Why Awakening Is Difficult for the Learned

Here's an uncomfortable truth: Awakening is often more difficult for those who are intellectually gifted.

Why?

Because the more we rely on thought, the harder it is to let go of it. The more we identify with knowledge, the more we resist the unknown. The mind seeks security in logic, but awakening requires surrender. A letting go of everything—even the need to understand.

The path is not about *adding* more—it's about *subtracting*. Removing the veil that clouds your true seeing.

So, What Is Awakening?

Awakening is a homecoming. A return to stillness, simplicity, and truth. It's the moment you realize you've been dreaming—and you wake up.

Not in theory, but in reality.

You see the world not as your mind interprets it—but as it *is*.

Pure. Unfiltered. Alive.

Final Thought: You Must Walk Through the Door Yourself

No one can do it for you. Not a teacher, not a philosophy, not even a divine being. They may show you the door. But you must walk through it yourself.

When you do, you'll discover that awakening was never far away.

It was always right here.

Inside you.

Waiting.

Chapter Fourteen

Wordless Door To Enlightenment

Most spiritual seekers come to the path not because life has been kind, but because it has left them yearning. They've explored many avenues—careers, relationships, knowledge, even conventional spiritual teachings—but somehow, satisfaction remains elusive. There is a nagging sense that something is missing, that life must hold more than this restless pursuit.

Our upbringing contributes greatly to this predicament. From a young age, we are trained to excel in grammar school, high school, and then college, following a system rooted in information and analysis. It's a journey guided by knowledge, but knowledge—by its very nature—is always partial. It dissects, labels, and categorizes, but never shows us the whole.

And herein lies the limitation: **knowledge may stimulate the mind, but it does not satisfy the heart.**

The **Diamond Sutra**, oracle of Buddhism, speaks directly to this truth. At the end of its 5,000 words, it concludes:

> "All actionable teaching is like a bubble and a dream, like the dew and the thunder."

In other words, meaning itself is impermanent—an illusion. What we cling to as truth or method is, in essence, transient and symbolic. That is why, throughout history, the greatest spiritual traditions have eventually moved beyond words into **wordless practice**, returning to direct experience.

Buddhism, after centuries of scriptures and teachings, evolved into something much simpler and more grounded. In many traditions, especially Mahayana and Zen, the path shifted toward **rituals of bowing, chanting, and silence**. These were not acts of performance, but of surrender—acts designed to humble the ego, engage the body, and open the heart. It is through these repetitive, reverent actions that the practitioner gradually dissolves the mental self and begins to taste pure presence.

Christianity, in its deepest essence, also moved away from dogma toward the **felt experience of divine love**. The teachings of Jesus emphasized childlike faith, trust in the Father, and unconditional love—not as theological abstractions but as living truths that had to be **felt, trusted, and surrendered to**. In its mystical branches, such as Christian contemplative prayer or monastic devotion, believers lose themselves in love, not logic. It is the **heart**—not the mind—that leads them to union with God.

When **Bodhidharma** brought **Buddhism to China**, something profound occurred. He encountered the ancient practices of **Taoism**, a tradition that already worked with the **body's meridians, energy flow, and internal alchemy**. The result was a merging of two paths—Buddhism's insight into emptiness and detachment, and Taoism's cultivation of internal life force. This marriage gave birth to **Chan Buddhism**, later known as **Zen**. Zen did not rely on scriptures or debate. It pointed directly to the **wordless transmission of truth**, often through paradox, stillness, breath, posture, and awareness of Qi. Meditation in this form was not purely mental—it was **energetic, somatic, and whole**.

These three great traditions—**Buddhism, Christianity, and Taoist-influenced Zen**—have endured not simply because of belief systems or written doctrine, but because they each found a way to **touch the human core without relying on the human intellect**. They discovered the same essential truth: that awakening must be lived, embodied, practiced—not merely understood.

They each found a **wordless door**—one that opens not with answers, but with presence.

Beyond Words: The Need for Direct Experience

True spiritual realization cannot be captured in language. What we need is a **wordless practice**—something that bypasses the analytical mind and touches the core of our being. This is why meditation has long been revered. But not all meditation is equal.

Particularly effective are practices rooted in the body—**chakra-based, meridian-focused meditations**. These engage not just the breath or the mind, but the **life force itself—Qi**. They work through energy pathways, awakening the body's innate intelligence. When Qi flows freely, we feel lighter, brighter, and more aligned with our physical well-being.

And from that physical satisfaction, something profound happens: **our spirit lifts**. Contentment in the body leads to contentment in the soul. The mind, once noisy with memories, projections, and reactions, begins to quiet. Not through force, but because it is overshadowed by a deeper sensation from the heart.

Stillness Is Not Enough: The Case for Motion Zen

However, stillness alone is not the end of the journey. Long hours of seated meditation can bring peace, yes—but also stagnation. The body, left motionless, begins to atrophy. Muscles weaken. The spine, our central axis of life force, may become misaligned. Pinched nerves and blocked meridians follow, sabotaging our well-being.

That's why we introduce **Motion Zen**—a practice of integrating stillness with movement. We strengthen the skeletal muscles to support proper alignment of the spine. We allow Qi to flow unimpeded through the meridians. We embody a living meditation, where each movement supports vitality, clarity, and sustainable contentment.

This is the path we offer—not a widely trodden road, but one that integrates **body, energy, and spirit**. A path not based on belief, but on experience. A path where knowledge steps aside, and life itself becomes the teacher.

May it serve you well.

Chapter Fifteen

A Path of No Path

Now that we have explored the fragmented nature of modern learning, it is clear that piecemeal knowledge—however sophisticated—fails to capture the full wonder of life. When we dissect nature into bits and pieces, we lose sight of its integrated beauty. We chase branches of knowledge and marvel at leaves, yet rarely do we see the whole tree. And even less often do we grasp its root.

This is not merely an intellectual problem—it is a spiritual one. The more we pursue knowledge as a collection of facts, the farther we move from the living truth of nature. The truth, as it reveals itself, is not something we can conquer, possess, or understand in the ordinary sense. In reality, **we can only flow with it**.

And so we flow.

All our earlier discussions on detachment have led us to a striking realization: **there is ultimately nothing to detach from.** The idea of detachment only makes sense if we believe there's something real, something solid, to hold on to. But as we've peeled back the layers, we've seen that much of what we cling to is illusory—shadows on the wall. Once this is understood, detachment becomes second nature, not a practice, but a living expression of inner clarity.

In the same way, we have come to recognize that the path forward cannot be divided into stillness **or** motion, internal **or** external. These dualities, while useful as teaching tools, ultimately dissolve into one unified dance. **Stillness and motion are not opposites. They are one.** Like breath and silence, like wind and sky—they arise together.

To live a life that is whole, one must practice both: the internal cultivation and the external flow. Without tending to both, we are like a tree with roots but no leaves, or leaves with no roots. We lose our balance. There is **no other path** but integration.

And in our exploration, we have identified the one universal connector that integrates and manifests every being in the universe.

Qi — the life force.

It is the only known energy that pulses through both body and spirit. Qi does not belong to any religion or philosophy. It is the energy of **life itself, internal and external**.

Through observing Josh—a child who lives unburdened by strategies or judgments—we have seen this life force in action. Josh does not think about love. He **is** love in motion. He does not analyze energy. He is driven by it. His joy, his curiosity, his adaptability—all arise from an **internal force** that flows freely, unblocked and untamed. He accepts each moment without resistance, without the need to plan, to control, or to grasp. In him, we see a mirror of what we've forgotten.

And maybe, just maybe... **this is the path.**

Maybe it's not about fixing every problem, solving every question, or chasing every answer. Maybe it's about working with the life force already within us—allowing it to strengthen our bodies, expand our awareness, and release us from the constant interruptions of our mind.

Maybe it's about letting go—not as an act of surrender, but as a natural consequence of being deeply **alive**.

In the chapters to come, I will share with you practices, reflections, and methods that have helped me reconnect with this energy. These are not doctrines. These are doorways—simple experiences that can help guide you back to your own wholeness.

I don't claim to have all the answers. But I do know this:

When the life force is flowing freely, health arises. Joy arises. Gratitude arises.

And life—life becomes the teacher.

Let us begin.

Part II

The Zen Lineage

Chapter Seventeen

The Origin Of Zen

One day, on the spiritual mountain of Vulture Peak, the Buddha was about to give a sermon to a large assembly of disciples, monks, and celestial beings. Instead of speaking, he simply sat in silence.

The crowd waited patiently, expecting him to begin his teaching with words. But the Buddha did something unexpected. He gently held up a single, beautiful flower—a golden lotus—and twirled it in his fingers.

He said not a single word.

The assembly was confused. They looked at the flower, then at each other, trying to decipher the hidden meaning of this silent gesture. They could not understand what the Buddha was trying to teach.

However, one monk in the crowd, Mahakasyapa (or in Pali, Mahakassapa), a senior disciple of the Buddha, looked at the flower and the Buddha's face, and a gentle smile broke across his own face. In that moment of silent communion, he understood perfectly.

Seeing Mahakasyapa's smile, the Buddha smiled back. He then addressed the assembly:

> "I possess the true Dharma eye, the marvelous mind of Nirvana, the true form of the formless, the subtle Dharma gate that does not rest on words or letters but is a special transmission outside of the scriptures. This, I now entrust to Mahakasyapa."

The Meaning and Significance

This story is incredibly important, especially in Zen Buddhism, for several reasons:

1. **Wordless Transmission:** It signifies that the deepest truths (Dharma) cannot be fully captured by words, intellectual explanations, or scriptures. True understanding is transmitted directly from mind to mind, heart to heart.

2. **Direct Experience:** The Buddha was pointing to the nature of reality itself—pure, undivided, and immediate. Mahakasyapa didn't **think** about the flower; he *experi-*

enced the teaching directly, beyond thought. He saw the flower's suchness, its perfection, and his own true nature reflected in it.

3. **The Origin of Zen:** This event is considered the founding moment of the Zen lineage. Mahakasyapa is regarded as the first Indian patriarch in a direct line of transmission that eventually spread to China by Bodhidarma. Bodidharma lived in a cave behind the Shaolin Temple for 9 years, before he began his teaching. Due to the proximity of the Shaolin Temple, Bodhidharma incorporated many Taoists practices into his teaching, such as Qigong and other meridian based practices. These unique practices were later named as "Chan", and later on, was taught in Japan (as Zen). Due to this unique integration, Bodhidarma is considered by many as the first patriarch of Zen, As you may know, Taoist practices share the same roots and principles with the traditional Chinese medicine.

4. **The Importance of Presence:** The story is a lesson in being fully present. While others were lost in confusion and intellectualizing, Mahakasyapa was simply present and open, allowing transmission to dawn.

In essence, the Buddha was not holding up a "flower." He was holding up the entire universe, the nature of mind, and the state of enlightenment itself—all of which are right here, right now.

Modern Scientific Perspective

Some call this a heart-to-heart transmission; others may call it a mind-to-mind synchronization. In modern science, this is simply message transmission, or resonance. Either way, it requires energy to be able to execute.

Like every sentient being in our world, we live on an energy platform. It is the essential current that powers us to eat, work, think, and be happy. Without it, nothing would be alive. This same energy is the medium for our deepest connections. It fuels not only our biological functions but also the invisible bridges of understanding we build between one another—whether through words, a shared glance, or a moment of silent resonance.

Chapter Eighteen

The Heart-to-Heart Transmission of Zen

As mentioned in the previous chapters, the Zen school's origin at the Vulture Peak assembly, where the Buddha held up a golden lotus flower, fully illustrates that its transmission has never relied on scriptures or words. It is a direct transmission from heart to heart, a silent understanding beyond language. My master, **Zen Master Wu Jue Miao Tian**, is the 85th-generation patriarch in the lineage stemming from **Shakyamuni Buddha**. He is the 58th patriarch since **Bodhidharma** brought Zen to China, and also the 48th patriarch of the **Linji (Rinzai) school**.

Despite this ancient and venerable history, my master's teachings are conveyed in remarkably modern language. For instance, when asked, **"What is Zen?"** he says:

> **"Zen is the universal life force of all sentient beings, wisdom and** manifestation.**"**

Doesn't that sound akin to the concept of God's power or the force of Nature? This definition points to the fundamental, generative energy that permeates all existence.

The Eight-Character Essence: Purity, Wisdom, Perfection, Complete Enlightenment

Master spent the first twenty years of his teaching primarily transmitting just eight characters. These four concepts form a progressive path of spiritual cultivation:

1. **Purity (Qīngjìng):** This is the essential foundation. It refers not to physical cleanliness but to a state of mental and spiritual clarity, free from the pollution of wandering thoughts, attachments, and afflictions (greed, anger, delusion, arrogance, and doubt). Through meditation, the mind settles, like mud sinking in still water, revealing its inherently pure nature.

2. **Wisdom (Zhìhuì):** From a state of purity,

our innate, intuitive wisdom—known as *Prajna*—naturally arises. This is not intellectual knowledge but the ultimate wisdom that perceives the true nature of reality. It is the direct insight that cuts through all illusion.

3. **Perfection (Yuánmǎn):** As this wisdom fully blossoms, practitioners realize that their innate nature is already complete and lacking nothing. It is a state of holistic fulfillment, understanding that the inner self (the microcosm) is intrinsically one with the entire universe (the macrocosm). Where both inner duties as well as external duties are to be fulfilled, resolving all karma.

4. **Complete Enlightenment (Yuánjué):** This is the ultimate fruit of practice—supreme, perfect awakening, or Buddhahood. It is the state of absolute freedom, liberation from the cycle of birth and death, and the complete realization of one's true nature.

These eight characters map the journey from cause (cultivating purity) to effect (achieving enlightenment).

The Rigorous Method of Zen Meditation: Aligning Body, Breath, and Mind

The practice of sitting meditation (*Zuo Chan*) in our tradition is exceptionally rigorous and precise.

- **Posture:** One must sit either in a half-lotus or full-lotus position on the floor. The **back must be perfectly straight**, aligning the spine. For the first three months, I spent almost every day just "practicing leg flexibility" and learning to sit correctly, not truly meditating. It was years later that I understood the critical reason: a straight spine allows for the smooth flow of **energy (Qi)** through the meridians. This correct alignment allows the **autonomic nervous system** to function optimally, inducing a state of deep calm and heightened awareness.

- **The Practice of Jiuzhuan Xiangong :** Furthermore, one must completely master a specific energy circulation practice known as **Jiuzhuan Xiangong (The Nine Revolutions Profound**

Practice). The sole purpose of this intense focus is to **completely dissolve the interference of the egoic self**—the constant chatter of the conscious mind, as well as restore health of our body. We do not count breaths or visualize images, as those are still activities of the conscious mind. By focusing all attention single-pointedly on the circulation of energy, we **utterly relinquish all conscious activity**. This creates the conditions necessary for the **heart-to-heart transmission** to occur.

The Unspoken Transmission: Experience Beyond Text

The teachings of the scriptures can easily be passed down through texts. However, the transmission of the **actual method—the "gongfu"** —has always primarily been through **personal demonstration and oral instruction** from master to disciple. This is likely why, even 700 years later, a revered master like **Zen Master Dōgen** who brought Zen (Soto) to Japan, may not have had the com-

plete transmission of this specific energetic practice system, focusing mostly on the profound philosophical and
"just sitting" (*Shikantaza*) aspects.

My Personal Experience: Knowing with the Heart, Not the Head

The Zen I have experienced is not something to be **understood with the intellectual brain or memorized
from past teachings.** One must **put the brain down
and use the heart to perceive and feel.** By sensing the
universe within one's own body—the flow of energy and
life force—one can resonate and become one with the
universe outside. This is the true meaning of **"One is all,
and All is One"**. It is a direct, experiential truth, not a
philosophical concept.

Chapter Nineteen

Distant from All Forms

Many of you have probably heard the word **Zen**. That is simply the Japanese pronunciation of the Chinese word **Chan** (C-H-A-N), as recorded in Wikipedia and many sources.

After three decades immersed in the practice and study of Chan—spending countless hours deciphering the **Diamond Sutra**, the **Heart Sutra**, and receiving direct guidance from my teacher—I have come to see that the essence of his teaching can be distilled into two profound practices:

1. **Distant from all Forms**

2. **Live Out Detachment**

These are not academic concepts. They are not religious dogmas or abstract philosophies. They are lived truths, cultivated in silence, tested in everyday life, and realized through deep, patient awareness.

Part I: The Practice of Distant from Forms

In Chinese, the word for form is **(Xiang)**—it refers to anything that has an appearance, a shape, a structure, or a traceable pattern. The term goes far beyond physical objects. "Form" includes:

- The air we breathe,

- The the person we met.

- The event in front of us.

- The thoughts that flash through our mind,

- The judgment in our mind,

- The words we read and speak,

- The logic we cling to,

- Even the sacred scriptures and teachings themselves.

Yes, even this book you are reading now is a *form*. And my teacher's teachings are forms too.

I remember clearly—in my early years of practice, filled with curiosity and reverence—I once asked my teacher:

"Is your teaching also a form?"

He didn't hesitate for a second.

"Yes, of course," he said.

That answer shattered something inside me—a stubborn belief that "form" only applied to mundane objects, not to the noble spiritual path.

What Distant Truly Means

Let us be very clear:

Distant from form does not mean rejecting form.

- It does not mean ignoring, abandoning, or erasing it.

- Instead, it means taking a step back, **not being bound or disturbed by form**.

- To be distant is to encounter form with full presence, but without entanglement.

- To accept it, recognize it, even embrace it—yet not be swayed by it.

- To understand it is the result of vast, unknowable chains of **cause and effect**.

- Form is not an enemy. Form is not a trap.

Form is simply what arises—what the law of cause and effect naturally unfolds. We don't have to fight it, deny it, or dive endlessly into "why."

A Personal Illustration of Karma

To illustrate the subtle yet powerful influence of cause and effect, let me share a story from my own life.

People often tell me, "You're so mild-tempered, so even-hearted."

What they don't know is **why** I became that way.

My father was a tyrant.

An authoritarian.

Unreasonably strict, often violent.

If I dared to speak back, I risked being beaten. I learned early on to suppress, to endure, to stay calm.

Why was he like that? Because **his mother—my grandmother—spoiled him terribly**. He grew up as an entitled, pampered boy who never heard the word "no."

Why did she raise him that way? Because she herself was from a wealthy, gentle, highly sheltered family. A kind woman, raised in comfort, unable to discipline him firmly.

See the pattern?

My mildness wasn't something noble or cultivated. It was the downstream result of **a chain of inherited causes and effects**, echoing across generations.

And that's just my small family. Multiply that by thousands of factors—social, historical, cultural—and you realize:

We are living manifestations of millions of causes.

Accept, Don't Resist

So when a form arises—a reaction, a personality trait, a trauma, a belief—don't fight it.

Accept it. Observe it. Fulfill it.

- It's not about resignation, but resolution.

- Detachment is not indifference. It is clarity.

- It is not seeing the form as a wave, but the entire ocean.

- It's not "giving up." It's "not being owned."

Part II: The Practice of Living Out Detachment

Understanding detachment intellectually is one thing.

But Zen is not a theory. Zen is life.

Real understanding must go beyond the mind.

It must be **embodied**—lived, practiced, expressed in motion, stillness, speech, silence, joy, and suffering.

My teacher used to say,

"Don't take notes. You don't need to understand it. Just live it."

You don't need to analyze every detail of cause and effect.

You don't need to perfect your knowledge.

You simply need to walk the path, moment by moment, without attachment to form.

- If a person insults you, it's a form.

- If praise arises, that too is form.

- If illness visits, or healing comes, both are forms.

- If fear knocks, let it knock. If peace arises, let it pass.

Do not let these forms affect your health.

Do not let them disturb your mind.

Detachment—Until It Becomes You

In the lineage of Chinese Chan (Zen), detachment is not something to be talked about or admired from afar. It is not an idea, a concept, or even a technique. It is a way of being. One must *practice out* detachment—not just understand it, but *live it out*, embody it, breathe it—until it becomes second nature. Or, in the deeper Buddhist sense, until it becomes your **self-nature**.

This is the turning point where practice is no longer something you do, but something you integrates with your heart.

When detachment reaches this depth, it no longer requires reminders or reinforcement. There is no more inner tug-of-war between letting go and holding on, between what you think should be and what is. Detachment then flows through your actions like water finds its path down a mountain—*naturally, effortlessly, without resistance.*

At this stage, **there is no more analyzing**. No more strategizing, plotting, or planning for the sake of control or outcome. It is not that you become careless; rather, you become **care-free**—freed from the chains of conceptual burdens. You no longer live from the mind's tight grip of evaluation and prediction, but from a clarity that rises from within—clear, unshakable, responsive.

As my teacher once said,

> "When detachment becomes your self-nature, even the concept of form no longer surfaces."

You walk, you speak, you act—yet none of it is born from calculation. There is no sense of "I am practicing detachment" or "I should let this go." There is simply an unbroken stream of presence, moving through time and space without clinging, without resisting.

In this clarity, **wisdom flows out of you unprovoked**, like the fragrance of a flower in bloom. You don't try to be wise, you don't perform insight. You have returned to the simplicity of your original nature. What remains is a profound stillness that lives even in movement, and a compassionate strength that does not rely on control.

This is the Zen of detachment—not retreating from life, but **being fully in it without being entangled by it**.

When this becomes your rhythm, even the distinction between detachment and attachment dissolves. There is no longer a watcher watching for detachment. There is only *living*—whole, grounded, empty, full.

Chapter Twenty

Stillness and Motion are One

Now, let us discuss how to sustain detachment and live it out.

My Chinese Chan master taught me something very important.

"There is stillness in motion, and there is motion in stillness."

It is so, because there are **two key parts** to Chinese Chan practice:

- **Sitting Zen (Sitting Chan)**

- **Motion Zen (Motion Chan)**

These two approaches may look different, but at their core, they are both powered by the **same essential element**:

> **Energy — life force, qi, the power of life, power of wisdom and power of manifestation.**

Sitting Zen: Stillness on the Outside, Energy Moving Within

In sitting Zen, the practitioner looks motionless on the outside.

But inside, they are **deeply engaged** with the energy systems of the body.

The practice works with:

- The meridians (energy pathways)

- The chakras (energy centers)

- The flow and circulation of **qi** (vital energy)

As the practice deepens, something profound happens:

- You lose the sensation of the physical body.

- The usual awareness of your torso, limbs, and

flesh **dissolves**.

- All that remains is the sense of energy — a living, flowing presence that fills and replaces the whole body.

This is why we say: **sitting Zen is quiet on the outside, but full of motion on the inside**.

Motion Zen: Motion on the Outside, Stillness Within

Motion Zen, on the other hand, looks like movement — Taichi, Yoga, Ba Duan Jin.

But inside, the practitioner maintains **deep stillness** and focused awareness.

Here, too, energy plays a key role.

- Your movements must be guided and aligned by internal focus.

- You detach from external distractions and turn inward, concentrating on the balance, rhythm, and flow of your motion.

- Gradually, the mechanical awareness of the body

moving fades, and you enter a state where only presence remains.

This is why we say: **motion Zen is moving on the outside, but still on the inside**.

The Unifying Element: Energy Is the Heart of Zen

My teacher emphasized a truth that I want to underline here clearly:

In both sitting meditation and motion meditation, **energy** is not optional — it is fundamental.

Once I asked my teacher, "What is Chan?" He answered:

Chan is the power of life force, the power of wisdom, and the power of manifestation.

- Without energy, there can be no life to live.

- Without energy, there can be no realization to be transmitted.

- Without energy, there can be no world to dwell.

As my teacher Wujue Miaotian said:

"Without Qi, it is a withered Chan."

This means that Zen is not just an intellectual exercise of the mind.

It is about engaging, cultivating, and integrating the vital energy that makes all things possible.

Energy is the fundamental bricklayer, the foundation upon which the teachings of Zen stand.

Whether you sit or move, it is this **living energy** that fuels the practice and opens the path.

Beyond Sitting and Moving

In the later chapters and appendix, we will introduce detailed lineage sitting Zen practices — focusing on how to guide energy through your body's internal networks.

In another book:

Qi – the platform for everything

we will explore motion Zen in detail.

But remember:

Both sitting Zen and Motion Zen are only tools.

Both point toward the same ultimate experience — a state where the heart is focused on lifeforce, the mind disappears, effort dissolves, and you arrive at what the ancient masters called **Wu Wei (Taoism)**:

Effortless being.

Pure awareness.

The merging with universal consciousness.

Chapter Twenty-One

The Universal Life Force: Qi

I n today's world, we often think of the physical and the spiritual as two separate realms. The physical is what we can see, touch, measure—the body, the earth, time, and space. The spiritual is what we sense but cannot grasp—awareness, intuition, purpose, insight. But ancient traditions saw no such divide. Instead, they spoke of something subtle yet essential that flows through both: **Qi**.

Pronounced "chee," Qi is often translated as *life force* or *vital energy*. But these words barely scratch the surface. In traditional Chinese medicine, Taoist philosophy, and martial arts, **Qi is the animating power behind all living things**. It flows through your breath, your thoughts, your blood, your presence. It is what makes you alive—not just biologically, but emotionally, mentally, spiritually.

And here's the key:

> **Without Qi, nothing moves. Nothing awakens. Nothing grows.**

What Is Qi? A Gentle Introduction

You don't have to be spiritual or believe in ancient texts to understand Qi. You've already felt it.

- When you take a deep breath after stress and feel clarity return—that's Qi moving.

- When a walk in nature resets your mood—that's Qi replenishing.

- When a heartfelt conversation leaves you feeling uplifted—that's Qi connecting.

It's not magic. It's not mysticism. It's the subtle energy behind everything that feels *real* but can't be held in your hand.

Western science might call it bioelectricity, metabolism, neural signaling, or cellular vibration. But in essence, **Qi is the fuel for both your physical body and spirit**. It's what allows your body to move, your mind to think, and your heart to feel. It fuels not just your heartbeat, but your joy. Not just your digestion, but your insight.

In later chapters, we will introduce you to a practical method that allows you to directly experience the flow of Qi in your own body—an energizing practice rooted in both tradition and personal vitality.

Qi: The Fundamental Thread of Life

Qi is not simply part of life—it **is** life. It is the underlying force that animates both the physical world and the spiritual dimension.

Without Qi:

- **The body** would be inert. Movement, growth, healing, all would halt.

- **The senses** would fall silent. No sight, no sound, no touch would register.

- **Awareness** would become blind. No insight, no intuition, no clarity could arise.

- **Wisdom** would have no carrier. Like a message

with no voice.

Every breath you take, every sensation you experience, every realization you come to—**all depend on the flow of Qi**. It is the current that powers both your biology and your consciousness.

In ancient thought, Qi connects *Rupa* (form) and *Nama* (name)—matter and spirit. It is what allows the formless to take shape and the shaped to dissolve into stillness. Without Qi, there is only stasis. With Qi, the dance of life begins.

In applying Qi to our health, the classic medical text Huangdi Neijing states: This is commonly translated as:

"When righteous Qi exists within, pathogenic Qi cannot invade."

This principle highlights the core of preventive medicine in Chinese thought. It tells us that by cultivating strong, vibrant internal Qi—especially Yang Qi, the active and warming aspect of energy—we create a kind of energetic immunity. (We will publish another book detailing TCM practices, such as Yang Qi.)

This is not only about defending against illness, but about using the **power of intention** to awaken and direct Qi toward vitality. When we focus our intention with clarity and trust in the body's natural intelligence, we activate internal healing processes. In this way, Qi becomes not just energy, but a *conscious force*, revitalizing every cell and restoring harmony from within.

The Body: A Platform for Both Worlds

In many spiritual traditions, the body is often treated as a hindrance or something to be transcended. But in Chinese and Taoist teachings, **the body is sacred**, because it is the **platform through which Qi flows**. And through Qi, it becomes the meeting ground of both the material and the spiritual.

The body is not just flesh and bone. It is a living, breathing energy system. Every joint, every breath, every heartbeat is part of a complex current. The more we support this current—through mindful movement, nourishing food, rest, and emotional clarity—the more open we become to wisdom, peace, and deep spiritual insight.

This is why disciplines like Tai Chi, Qigong, acupuncture, and breathwork focus not just on muscles or posture, but on **restoring the smooth flow of Qi**. They are not just health practices—they are gateways to aligning body and spirit.

Living in Alignment: When Qi Flows Freely

When Qi flows:

- The body becomes light, agile, and energized.

- The mind becomes clear, grounded, and present.

- The spirit becomes open, connected, and wise.

There is no longer a wall between the physical and the spiritual. You begin to feel them as one continuous experience. Eating a meal becomes a sacred act. Walking becomes meditation. Listening becomes compassion.

This is not about escaping the world. It is about **being so fully alive** that every moment pulses with meaning.

The Energy That Awakens Everything

Qi is not just the thread that connects body and spirit. It is the **weaving itself**—the animating intelligence of life. Without it, time does not move, growth does not happen, senses do not register, and wisdom has no path to travel.

The physical world needs Qi to grow and heal.

The spiritual world needs Qi to awaken.

And both need the **body** as the platform through which Qi can flow freely.

In a later chapter on consciousness, we will also explore the ancient Chinese concept of the Three Treasures—Jing, Qi, and Shen—as presented in the classic Huangdi Nei-jing. You will see how Qi sits at the heart of this trinity, linking physical vitality with the rise of consciousness itself.

The more we care for our Qi, the more whole we become.

As an old Zen teaching reminds us:

> "Before enlightenment, chop wood, carry water. After enlightenment, chop wood, carry water."

Chapter Twenty-Two

Consciousness — Where Science, Ancient Wisdom, and TCM Meet

What is consciousness?

I s it merely the flickering activity inside the brain? A dance of neurons, chemicals, and electrical patterns?

Or is it something far deeper — the integrated flow of mind, heart, body, and spirit?

For centuries, humans have sought to understand the mystery of awareness. While modern science explains consciousness through the lens of biology, ancient traditions across cultures have long described it as a layered, living essence.

In this chapter, we will explore how:

Modern neuroscience,

Ancient spiritual teachings, and

Traditional Chinese medicine (TCM)

converge on one profound realization:

We cannot reach higher, universal consciousness without grounding ourselves in the strength and vitality of the physical body.

Section 1: Modern Science — A System-Wide Phenomenon

Neuroscience traditionally placed consciousness in the brain, mapping areas like the **cerebral cortex**, **thalamus**, and **reticular activating system** as key players in awareness.

But today, science is expanding its understanding.

- **Heart-Brain Communication**:

- The heart has its own neural network, the "heart brain," sending more signals to the brain than the brain sends to it. Emotional states — like love, gratitude, and peace — create coherent heart rhythms, improving brain function.

- **Embodied Mind**:

- Consciousness is not confined to the skull. Gut bacteria, immune responses, and skin sensors feed signals back to the brain, shaping mood, decision-making, and perception. This is called **embodied cognition**.

Key Point: Science now recognizes that consciousness is a system-wide, body-wide process. Physical states directly shape mental clarity and emotional resilience.

Section 2: Ancient Spiritual Teachings — Heart and Spirit in Alignment

Across traditions — Buddhism, Taoism, Christian mysticism, Sufism — we find a shared understanding:

The mind alone cannot reach higher truths. The heart must open, and the spirit must awaken.

- **Buddhism** speaks of fluid, impermanent consciousness (*vijñāna*), shaped by perception and intention.

- **Taoism** emphasizes that true knowing arises from the heart (*xin*), not the analytical mind.

- **Christian mystics** describe the heart as the place of direct communion with the divine.

- **Sufism** speaks of the *qalb*, the polished heart reflecting divine light when ego and attachments are cleared.

Key Point: Without the alignment of heart, mind, and spirit, consciousness remains clouded.

Section 3: Chinese Medicine — The Three Treasures of Jing, Qi, Shen

The *Huangdi Neijing*, the foundational text of Chinese medicine, offers a brilliant framework:

The Three Treasures — Jing, Qi, Shen.

- **Jing (Essence):**

- Your inherited life-force, stored in the kidneys.

This is your body's *battery* — the deep reservoir of energy that governs growth, reproduction, and longevity. It has a finite capacity.

- **Qi (Vital Energy):**

- The dynamic life-force circulating through meridians, nourishing every organ and system. Qi is the **electricity** drawn from the battery to power the body.

- **Shen (Spirit / Consciousness):**

- The radiant spirit, the spark of awareness, perception, and higher consciousness. Shen is the **light** that shines forth — but it depends on the strength of Jing and the ample flow of Qi.

In Layman's terms

Let me put it simply.

Your **Jing** — or essence — is like your body's deep energy reserve, like a battery pack that slowly drains over time. It's not something you can easily refill. Every day you live, think, move, or stress out, you're using a little bit of this battery.

Now, when you're **really tired**, so exhausted you just want to collapse into bed and don't care about anything else — that's a sign your body doesn't have enough **Qi**, your daily energy, to keep you going. And that's because your Qi is supplied by your **Jing**. If there's not enough Jing to draw from, the Qi drops, and your **Shen** — your awareness, your ability to think clearly, focus, and feel inspired — dims too.

But when you've had a really **good night's sleep**, you wake up feeling fresh, alert, and like you can take on the world. That's because your body was able to convert some Jing into Qi while you were resting, giving you enough fuel to power your awareness.

This shows two important things:

1. Your **awareness and mental state depend on the available Qi** in your system.

2. And **Qi comes from your internal essence — your Jing — not from absorbing energy out of thin air or the universe.**

That's why **extreme sports**, overworking, or constantly pushing yourself can age you faster. You're burning through your Jing — your life's core energy — too quickly. And once it's gone, it's hard to replace.

So instead of always trying to "push through," learn to **rest, nourish, and preserve** your essence. That's the real key to lasting energy and clarity.

Crucial Insight:

If the Jing is depleted, or the Qi blocked, the Shen dims.

Without strong physical health and balanced energy, consciousness cannot fully flourish.

Most spiritual teachings take this for granted — they speak of mind and spirit but often overlook the body as the **foundation** of awareness.

Section 4: A Unified Perspective — Consciousness as Embodied Awakening

When we bring together modern science, ancient spirituality, and Chinese medicine, we see:

- **Modern science** reveals the body's influence on mental and emotional states.

- **Ancient teachings** show the heart's central role in awakening.

- **Chinese medicine** reminds us that without physical vitality, the spirit cannot shine.

Core Message:

To reach universal consciousness, you must first care for the vessel — your body.

Physical health, energetic balance, and emotional harmony create the fertile ground where higher awareness can grow.

Consciousness is not an escape from the body; it is the flowering of life itself, supported by the body's strength.

Section 5: Practical Path — Cultivating Jing, Qi, and Shen

To harmonize body and spirit:

- **Nourish Your Jing:**

- Achieve deep, restorative sleep; avoid overexertion; and preserve your vital essence through balanced living. Or try some practice that can directly nourish your vital essence, which we will discuss in later chapters.

- **Circulate Your Qi:**

- Practice gentle, flowing movements like Qigong, Tai Chi, or Motion Zen to unblock your meridians and uplift your energy.

- **Brighten Your Shen:**

- Cultivate heart-centered emotions (gratitude, compassion); practice "neti neti"; focus on your energized, high spirited body.

Remember: The brilliance of your Shen — your spirit, your consciousness — arises from the strength of your Jing and the vitality of your Qi. Both are components of your body.

Critical Awareness - Focus

Consciousness is not a disembodied phenomenon; it is the living dance of body, energy, and spirit.

The body is the root, Qi is the flow, and Shen is the flower.

Without a strong foundation, the highest awareness cannot bloom.

Now that we understand the need for a **strong energy platform** — the Jing (essence) and Qi (vital energy) — to support Shen (consciousness), a new realization emerges:

Consciousness does not exist in isolation.

It can arise from many different sources: our sensory experiences, our emotional responses, our scattered thoughts, our egoic impulses, and — when properly focused — from the universal, expansive field beyond the individual self.

Many spiritual teachers compare consciousness to a **flashlight**.

Wherever you point it, that's where the light connects.

If we allow the flashlight of our awareness to constantly flicker between egoic desires, social anxieties, and random mental noise, then our consciousness becomes **fragmented, distracted, and drained**.

But — and here's the key —

We can train where we direct that beam.

We can consciously choose to focus our awareness not on the petty disturbances of daily life, but on something much larger: the energy of life itself, the vibrancy of a healthy body, the harmonized rhythms of mind, heart, and breath.

When we **focus on the pleasures of a spirited, energized, joyful body**,

we create a natural state with our *heart* that:

- Overshadows the worrying mind,

- Quietens the wandering thoughts,

- Dissolves random flashes of distraction.

In other words, physical vitality becomes a gateway, a **launchpad** for expanding awareness outward — beyond the narrow self — and connecting to **universal consciousness**.

Instead of sitting endlessly, meditating without clear direction, or practicing techniques in isolation, we must first cultivate the foundation: a vibrant, energetic body and harmonized Qi. Only then can our consciousness expand toward the universal, beyond the ego, into true alignment with the great field of life naturally.

This is the natural integrated path:

Build the body (Jing),

Harmonize the energy (Qi),

Illuminate the spirit (Shen),

Direct the awareness outward toward the universal, not inward toward egoic loops.

By bringing together modern science, ancient spiritual wisdom, and the timeless teachings of Chinese medicine, we learn:

Consciousness is not about striving; it is about fully entering the embodied dance of life, maximizing body, energy, and spirit, and focusing awareness everywhere and nowhere.

This is how we awaken naturally.

This is how we connect naturally.

This is how we return home to the universal consciousness naturally.

Chapter Twenty-Three

Clarifying the Language of Inner Functions

A Reflection on Heart, Brain, and Spirit

Throughout my years of teaching and practicing, I've encountered many sincere seekers—some trained in Japanese Zen, others rooted in Buddhist study, and many influenced by New Age thinking. Each carried a slightly different understanding of the inner workings of what we commonly call the "mind." Some spoke of "heart-mind." Others insisted it was simply "mind." But few could define it clearly, and even fewer agreed with one another.

In English, the word **mind** is a slippery thing. It tries to include everything—from thoughts and feelings, to awareness and memory—but in doing so, it becomes vague and confusing. It tries to hold too much in one word. When translated into Chinese, there is no direct equivalent. Is it □ (*xin*, heart)? □ (*yi*, intent)? □ (*shen*, spirit)? □ (*nao*, brain)? All of them point to something real, but none of them alone fully captures what "mind" tries to cover.

So before I take you any further into deeper waters—into the discussion of awareness, realization, or transformation—I feel it is only kind to clarify how I use these words: **heart, brain, and spirit**. Each, in my teaching, is not a vague idea but a **functional space**. A distinct activity center with its own strengths and limitations. Like three instruments in the same orchestra—each one contributes its own sound to the music of our being.

The Heart: The Feeling Field

When I say *heart*, I do not mean the biological organ. Nor do I mean emotions alone. The heart, in this context, is the **field of direct feeling**. It is where peace is felt. Where joy arises. Where sorrow resides quietly. The heart cannot remember. It does not calculate. It does not compare. It cannot analyze. And yet, it knows.

The heart has no past and no future. It does not live in time. It simply *feels* the present, intimately, without distance. This is why we often say: "Follow your heart." Because the heart does not lie. It may not explain itself—but it is honest.

The Brain: The Machine of Logic

The *brain* is a marvel of nature. It can memorize entire volumes, solve equations, analyze outcomes, and discriminate between choices. It is a powerful servant—but a poor master.

The brain stores memory. It retrieves information. It draws conclusions based on past data. But it does not feel. It can simulate feelings with great complexity, even convince you it knows happiness—but it does not *feel* happiness. That belongs to the heart.

The brain is essential for survival, but it is not the seat of wisdom. It can be trained. It can be brilliant. But brilliance without compassion is like a sword without a sheath—sharp, cold, and dangerous.

The Spirit: The Field of Awareness

The *spirit*—or *shen* (□) in Chinese—is the most subtle of the three. It is not a belief. It is not religious. It is simply the **field of pure awareness**. It observes. It knows. It does not interfere. It does not react. It simply *is*.

Spirit is what notices the thoughts of the brain and the feelings of the heart. It is the silent witness behind both. When we say someone is "present," we are often referring to this awakened spirit—fully here, fully aware, not caught in past or future.

Spirit is not a function of effort. You cannot "try" to be aware. Awareness simply is. Like the sky—unchanging behind the clouds.

Three Instruments, One Song

These three—heart, brain, spirit—are not separated in life. They affect one another, dance with one another, and sometimes conflict with one another. But for the sake of **clarity in practice**, I find it helpful to distinguish them.

This is not a philosophy. It is a pointing—a functional map to help you navigate your inner experience. Each part of your being has its role.

- Let the **heart** feel truth.

- Let the **brain** carry tools and analysis.

- Let the **spirit** remain still and clear, like a mirror.

Together, they form a complete human being. Together, they are the ground upon which all Zen practice can unfold—not through confusion, but through clarity.

If you don't know which one is speaking—pause. Breathe. Feel. Observe. That, too, is practice.

Would you like this formatted into a DOCX file or translated into Chinese in the same tone?

Part III

The Heart Practice

Chapter Twenty-Five

The Practice of Fulfillment

"We were all brought up to be somebody. But the path of fulfillment is to become everybody. And when you truly become everybody, you actually become nobody."

A New Beginning

In 2001, I found myself at the threshold of a new life. I had just begun my journey into Zen practice, filled with curiosity but weighed down by uncertainty. In one of my first teachings, I was introduced to four essential practices said to guide one toward enlightenment: **Purity, Wisdom, Fulfillment, and Enlightenment**.

Purity seemed like a mountain too high to climb—how could I possibly purify every thought, every impulse, every shadow of my mind? Wisdom, too, felt like a distant star—shining but unreachable. But *fulfillment*? That seemed like something I could try.

So I did.

The First Step: Saying Yes to the Plate

I chose the most concrete opportunity for practice—my own home, and specifically, my wife's kitchen. My wife has always cooked with health in mind: low salt, low oil, mostly vegetables. I, on the other hand, was raised in a traditional Shanghai family where food meant rich flavors, sugar-laced sauces, and dishes that lingered on your tongue with warmth and nostalgia.

Her cooking? Too light, too plain, too... healthy.

But I made a vow: I would eat every dish she prepared, without complaint, without alteration, without resistance.

At first, every meal felt like a practice in suffering. I missed the heavy sweetness of my childhood. Yet, as the months passed—one plate after another—I started to change. I began to notice a natural sweetness in the vegetables. The lightness of the meal left my body feeling clearer, more at ease. I realized: I was not just accepting her food—I was softening the grip of my preferences. Fulfillment had begun.

The Second Step: Saying Yes to Life

Encouraged by this inner shift, I expanded the practice.

What if I said **yes** to *everything* she asked of me?

"Can you wash the dishes?" she'd say—just as the baseball game reached its final pitch.

"Can you vacuum the floor?"—right in the climax of a mystery film.

Every request became a moment of truth. Each yes felt like a small defeat of the self—but also a quiet victory over ego.

At first, I gritted my teeth. For two years, I struggled. I wasn't just washing dishes—I was scrubbing away attachments. I wasn't just vacuuming—I was clearing the dust of old habits. And slowly, like mist lifting from the mountains, I began to see: the things I used to treasure—my little joys, my sacred preferences—weren't so important after all.

I was starting to be free.

Freedom in Obedience

Three years into this practice, I realized something beautiful and unexpected. My wife loved me more. But it wasn't because I did everything she asked. It was because I had stopped resisting. I had stopped being "me" and started becoming "us."

In that surrender, I wasn't losing myself. I was simply shedding the need to defend a self-image. By saying yes to everything, I no longer had to hold an opinion, form a judgment, or win an argument. I was no longer the man watching the game—I was the man who no longer needed the game to be fulfilled.

I became her. And clearly, we became one. There was no one left to oppose. There was no one left to blame.

There was only one.

Becoming Everybody, Becoming Nobody

When I shared this story with my students, many of them laughed and said, "I wish my spouse would practice that!"

I smiled and said gently, "This practice is not for your spouse. It's for *you*."

We were all brought up to be **somebody**. We were trained, from a young age, to build an identity, to achieve, to be noticed. But the path of spiritual fulfillment does not ask you to be special—it invites you to be **universal**.

We were all brought up to be somebody. But the path of fulfillment is to become everybody. And when you truly become everybody, you actually become nobody.

This is not a loss—it is a liberation. When there is no "you" to defend, there is no conflict. When there is no form to cling to, there is no suffering. You are free to be anything, to move with life, to be the sky instead of the cloud.

Try to say "yes" on small things first

Fulfillment is not about meeting expectations. It's about releasing the need to control, to be right, to be separate. It's about merging with what is—whether that's a meal, a task, or a moment.

You might begin this practice right now. Say yes to something you usually resist. Start small. It might be a meal. A chore. A conversation. Just say yes—and mean it. Don't fake it. Don't tolerate it. *Accept* it.

And observe what happens.

You may find that behind every "yes" is a doorway. And behind every doorway is a room you never knew existed: a room of peace, of spaciousness, of unshakable ease.

You are no longer a person defending their little world. You have become the world itself.

A Christian Parallel

In Christian teachings, there is also the path of surrender. And the essence is no different. True surrender in the Christian sense must be **total**, **complete**, and **immediate**—without hesitation. It is not partial, not calculated. It is a full offering of the self to God's will, just as the Zen path offers the self to the present moment. The forms may differ, but the spirit is the same.

Whether you call it surrender or fulfillment, the heart of the practice is the same: *the dropping of the ego*. And in that dropping, something greater arises—a life that is no longer yours alone, but shared with all that is.

This is the practice of saying yes. This is the practice of becoming nobody.

Chapter Twenty-Six

The Two Layers of Fulfillment

A Practice Misunderstood

In Buddhist teachings, few principles are as quietly powerful—and as widely misunderstood—as *fulfillment* and *harmonization*. These are not passive traits, nor signs of blind obedience. They are active practices, requiring clarity, courage, and a gradual dismantling of ego.

Most people associate fulfillment with doing one's duty—being a good parent, a loyal employee, a responsible citizen. Similarly, harmonization is often equated with getting along, keeping the peace, and avoiding conflict. These understandings only touch the **first layer** of the teaching.

In truth, **fulfillment and harmonization occur on two distinct levels**. The first is external; the second is internal. The first is visible; the second is profound. Until both levels are addressed, the practice remains incomplete.

Phase One: Outward Fulfillment, Inward Resistance

In the first phase, a person may fulfill their responsibilities with visible success. They may appear kind, cooperative, and accommodating. They play their role well. From the outside, everything seems harmonious. But within, **the ego still whispers**.

There is subtle resistance, quiet dissatisfaction. Regret. A sense of self-sacrifice. A lingering thought: *"Why do I have to give in? Why can't they change instead?"*

This is the **ego in disguise**—wearing a mask of agreement, while still clinging to its judgments. The mind complies, but the heart is unsettled. This creates a split between the **outer form** and the **inner truth**. One is fulfilled; the other is not.

This stage can last years. For some, a lifetime. Many confuse this surface harmony for spiritual maturity. But deep inside, they feel drained, unseen, or morally superior. That's how the ego survives—by objecting internally while smiling externally.

The Ego Test: A Humble Mirror

Want to know how big your ego still is?

Try this simple test.

The Spouse Test.

If your spouse calls you—right in the middle of the final seconds of your favorite sports game, or during the climax of a suspenseful movie—and asks you to do something...

Can you say **"Yes"** immediately, without hesitation?

Not a grudging yes. Not a delayed yes. Not a yes with a sigh.

But a cheerful, unhesitating, wholehearted yes—with immediate action.

If you can do that every time, congratulations:

You either have **a very small ego**—or none at all.

But if you hesitate, if your mind starts calculating, if resentment arises even slightly, then take it as a gentle bell—your ego is still holding court inside.

This is not a test about obedience. It's about **ego transparency**. About how quickly you can set yourself aside, how free you are from clinging to your own preference, even in a trivial moment.

That's the kind of moment where **real spiritual practice begins**.

The Turning Point: Recognizing the Ego's Echo

The shift begins the moment you start to **recognize the voice of ego**, not as your true self, but as a conditioned habit. You begin to see how it constantly objects, resists, compares, and demands acknowledgment.

At this stage, fulfillment becomes an inner practice. You start noticing when your actions are peaceful in form but conflicted in essence. You become aware of the **gap between your conduct and your consciousness**.

And most importantly, you begin to realize: **You have a choice.**

Not a choice between fighting or fleeing—but a choice to **observe**, to **release**, and to **diminish the ego's grip**. Every time the ego stirs up with resistance, you gently squash it—not by force, but with awareness. Not to destroy it, but to see through it.

This awareness is the quiet beginning of inner freedom.

Phase Two: Inward and Outward Completion

As the ego gradually diminishes, a new kind of fulfillment arises. One that is **complete**, both outwardly and inwardly. Your actions align with your awareness. Your service is not reluctant, but natural. You no longer struggle with "being right" or "being seen." You simply **respond to what is needed**.

Now, when you fulfill a duty, it feels light—because there's no residue. No inner protest. No sense of being diminished. Instead, there is joy, clarity, and a profound sense of **flow**.

When you harmonize with others, it's not from avoidance or compromise. It is from understanding. You no longer demand others to change before you find peace. You see clearly that their hindrances are not theirs alone—they arise from the artificial structures and belief systems we all share.

This is **true harmonization**: when your inner state matches your outer action. When your form reflects your spirit. When you are no longer performing harmony, but living it.

The Source of All Hindrance

Most conflicts—internal and external—arise not from nature, but from the artificial world of forms: identities, social roles, systems of comparison, and conditioned judgments.

The universe itself is never in conflict. It does not second-guess. It does not hurry. It fulfills itself in every moment—without ego, without resistance. **Nature never makes a mistake.**

As long as hindrances are human-made, they can be unmade. With access to **universal consciousness**, solutions arise that ego cannot conceive. You begin to *see through the form*—whether it's a label, a tradition, or an emotional reaction—and respond with what the situation *truly calls for*.

A Practice of Wholeness

Fulfillment and harmonization are not static states—they are living practices. At first, you fulfill roles outwardly, while wrestling with ego inwardly. Eventually, you begin to see your own resistance clearly, and gently dissolve it.

And finally, one day, your fulfillment becomes whole—externally clear and internally free. Your harmonization with nature is no longer a performance to be perfected, but a presence to be lived. You no longer need to prove, achieve, or practice. You simply are. And that is enough.

You move through life not by imposing will, but by embodying stillness. You act without regret. You respond without resistance. You serve without the need to be seen. In this state, you don't try to bring peace—you **are** peace. Not through effort, but through effortless being.

There is no ripple in your heart. No expectations of any sort. No hunger for outcomes or praise.

I remember once a student asked me, "If you have no desires, wouldn't life become boring?" I answered, "Until you reach this state of being, you won't understand how peaceful—and how **astonishingly liberating** —it is."

Every moment feels like a fresh reboot. Like the universe pressing the reset button just for you. Each moment is brand new. Light. Unburdened. Curious. Even brushing your teeth becomes a miracle. The wind on your face becomes a love letter. A falling leaf becomes a message from eternity.

You begin to notice: life doesn't stop surprising you. Not with loud fireworks, but with gentle whispers. A smile from a stranger. The dance of sunlight on the floor. The quiet comfort of your own breath.

And slowly, your heart overflows with gratitude—not the kind you say, but the kind you live. You thank everything, everyone, every breath—not because you were told to, but because you can't help it.

You become religious not in name, but in spirit. You bow—not out of duty, but out of awe. You surrender—not in defeat, but in reverence.

You are no longer the master of your life—you are its servant. A faithful steward of each beat, each blessing. You follow the rhythm of a higher will—not blindly, but joyfully. You become God's instrument, shaped by love, guided by light, moved by grace.

And in that surrender, you find the greatest freedom. You expect nothing. You cling to nothing. You fear nothing.

Because everything is already a gift.

And you—You are simply here.Surprised, grateful, and wholly at peace.

Chapter Twenty-Seven

Challenges in Harmonizing Body, Mind, and Spirit

E ach of us is a woven tapestry of three interconnected threads—the body, the mind, and the spirit (or heart). To achieve a true and enduring transformation, we must weave these threads together, nurturing each one in harmony. Focusing narrowly on just one aspect limits our growth, yet this is often the path most traveled in self-help and spiritual teachings.

The Problem with One-Dimensional Focus

Explore many books on spirituality, contentment, or happiness, and you will see a familiar pattern—they often speak exclusively to the mind. They guide us toward inward reflection, meditation, mindfulness, and letting go of external attachments. As Leo Babauta beautifully expressed in *The Little Book of Contentment*, **"Almost every kind of problem we have has discontent with ourselves (and our lives) as its root."** Yet even with this profound insight, such teachings rarely show us how to nourish the heart or energize the body directly.

Why the Body Matters

Why does this gentle oversight matter so much? Simply put, the body and heart profoundly shape the landscape of the mind. When your body is vibrant and alive, your heart lifts naturally, resonating joyfully with the rhythms of life. Energized and flowing, your body fills your being with dopamine and oxytocin—chemicals that bloom as happiness, warmth, and deep connection. In this radiant state, the mind calms effortlessly, anxiety melts away, and peaceful contentment blossoms naturally.

As Robert A. Johnson and Jerry M. Ruhl remind us in *Contentment: A Way to True Happiness*, **"Contentment comes from the inside."** Yet, the "inside" they speak of is not limited to mental landscapes; it embraces the whole of your being—your emotional depths and your body's vital energy.

Starting with the Tangible

Among the three intertwined threads of our existence, the body offers the most tangible, responsive starting point. Engaging directly with the mind can feel like grasping at clouds—thoughts are elusive, restless, and resistant to gentle control. But the body is present and palpable; you can feel it, move it, energize it. Its responsiveness provides clear, comforting feedback, encouraging you to deepen your practice and stay grounded in the present.

By caring for your physical form first, you establish a solid and true foundation. The heart rises naturally, buoyant and open. The mind then settles gracefully into harmony, drawn by the gentle rhythms of the energized body. This holistic dance of body, heart, and mind is the essence of genuine, lasting contentment.

Cultivating Awareness Through the Body

As Tracy Wilde-Pace tenderly advises in *Contentment: The Sacred Path to Loving the Life You Have*, cultivating true contentment **"takes time, practice, and an awareness."** And what better place to nurture this awareness than within your own body, where every sensation anchors you gently yet firmly in the present?

Looking Ahead

Ultimately, we advocate a balanced, poetic approach—beginning gently with the body, enriching the heart, and naturally soothing the mind. In the next chapter, we will guide you lovingly, step-by-step, on how to energize and revitalize your body. From this foundation, joy and peace will effortlessly flow upward, filling your heart and calming your mind. Rather than simply working hard on detachment, you will begin to experience it deeply, fully, and effortlessly.

The Brain and the Illusion of Sensory Reality

The human brain is a marvel of evolution—an intricate supercomputer wired to interpret the world through five primary senses: sight, sound, smell, taste, and touch. These sensory organs act as data collectors, feeding the brain a constant stream of information, which it then processes, categorizes, analyzes, compares, and judges—all in an instant. This system is automatic, relentless, and deeply rooted in survival. It allows us to distinguish a dollar bill from a ten-dollar bill, a red traffic light from a green one, the scent of danger from the fragrance of safety. Without it, navigating the physical world would be impossible.

Yet, for all its brilliance, this system has a fundamental flaw: **its inputs are limited, regional, and confined to the present moment.**

The Limits of Sensory Perception

Our senses operate within strict boundaries. How far can you see? Even with perfect vision, the horizon cuts off your perception. How far can you hear? A shout fades into silence beyond a certain distance. Our senses capture only fragments of reality—and worse, they perceive only **effects**, not causes.

When you see a tree, you do not see the seed that grew it decades ago. When you hear thunder, you do not hear the atmospheric conditions that created it. The senses present us with **current results**—snapshots of phenomena detached from their origins. The brain, however, treats these snapshots as complete truth, weaving them into a story based on memory and conditioning. But this story is incomplete.

The Trap of Naming and Categorizing

I recall in one of Eckhart Tolle's lectures, he held up a rose and offered a profound insight: *"This rose is to be appreciated for its beauty and fragrance—not to be named, categorized, or trimmed for your pleasure."* In that moment, he exposed a deep flaw in how we perceive reality.

The instant our senses detect something, the brain rushes to label it. *"Rose. Flower. Plant. Red. Pleasant smell."* Then come the judgments: *"This one is prettier than that one. It would look better in a vase. I should cut it and take it home."* In this way, we never truly experience the rose—we only experience our **thoughts about** the rose. The living reality of the flower is lost beneath layers of mental noise.

This is how we interact with nearly everything: not as it **is**, but as our brain **interprets** it. We mistake the label for the thing itself, the category for the truth.

The Blindness to Causes

Because our senses are regional and limited, they can only detect immediate events—the consequences of causes that may have been set in motion long ago. A war breaks out, but we do not perceive the centuries of tension that led to it. A person acts in anger, but we do not see the lifetime of pain that shaped them. The brain, relying solely on sensory input, reacts to the surface-level phenomenon without understanding the deeper forces at work.

The only way to **know the true causes** behind what we see and hear is to **transcend the immediate sensory data**—to visualize reality from a broader, even universal, perspective. Only then can we begin to recognize the hidden chains of causality that shape our world.

The Brain's Relentless Judgments

The brain does not merely observe—it judges. Every sensation is filtered through layers of memory, past experiences, biases, and survival instincts. A rustle in the bushes is instantly labeled "threat" or "harmless." A stranger's tone is categorized as "kind" or "hostile." These judgments are automatic, shaped by a lifetime of conditioning.

But what if those judgments are based on incomplete information? What if the brain is reacting to **effects** while remaining blind to their **true causes**? This is the great illusion of perception: we mistake the visible for the real, the immediate for the absolute.

The Prison of the Senses

We live in a world where we must respond to responsibilities, relationships, and external demands. Yet, if our perception is constrained by the senses—and our thoughts are dictated by the brain's automatic interpretations—how do we break free? How do we perceive the deeper truths that lie beyond the surface of things?

Scientific Discovery

Importantly, **science now validates** this mind-body-heart connection. As Dr. Martin Picard of Columbia University emphasizes, the **quantity and energy efficiency of mitochondria – especially in brain cells – is foundational to healthy brain function**. (see Appendix 8) In other words, your mental clarity, emotional regulation, and even perception of reality are deeply dependent on your body's cellular vitality.

So if you want to liberate your mind, start by **nourishing the power plants of your cells**. This is not just poetic – it is biological.

The journey continues as we explore how to awaken these deeper capacities within ourselves. For true clarity comes not from the brain alone, but from the **whole of our being** – body, heart, and mind in harmonious alignment.

This is the path to **real freedom of perception**.

Let us walk it together.

The Heart Has No Memory

Our heart has no memory.

It does not archive the past, nor does it project into the future.

It does not weigh the pros and cons, search for patterns, or build defenses. These are the mind's responsibilities — its habits, its coping mechanisms. But the heart plays a different role altogether.

The heart does not judge.

It does not compare, label, or analyze.

It does not ask whether something is right or wrong, better or worse, deserved or unfair.

Instead, the heart simply *feels*.

It feels the warmth of love, the ache of loss, the weight of sorrow, the joy of presence — without commentary, without filter. The heart experiences life directly, without translation.

To live with a pure heart is to return to this simplicity.

To strip away the conditioning, the mental noise, the inherited beliefs — and stand naked before each moment, undefended and whole.

In this space, love is not earned.

Compassion is not calculated.

Forgiveness is not a process — it is instant, because there is no memory to hold a grudge.

A pure heart lives in the *now*, without the clutter of what was or what might be.

And in this presence, something beautiful happens — we begin to feel life as it truly is.

We see others not as ideas or roles, but as fellow beings — raw, real, luminous.

The mind seeks control. The heart seeks connection.

The mind speaks of right and wrong. The heart whispers, "Are you hurting?"

The mind wants to win. The heart wants to hold.

This is not sentimentality. It is not weakness.

It is strength of the highest order — the courage to be fully human.

To feel everything. To judge nothing.

To love anyway.

The Spiritual Heart: Beyond Labels

In the world of spiritual teaching, countless labels are used to describe the invisible center within us: the **inner self**, **true nature**, **divine essence**, or **heart-mind**. Each term points toward the same experience — a state of love, compassion, peace, and profound stillness.

But these are just *labels*.

Each tradition or teaching chooses its own name. Some speak of Buddha-nature, some refer to the Christ within. Others use poetic language — soul, source, inner light. And while the words vary, the essence remains the same.

What they all attempt to describe is something that cannot be grasped or felt by the *brain*.

The brain is a tool of thought.

It can calculate, recall, reason, and compare.

But it cannot *feel* compassion.

It cannot *experience* peace.

It cannot *embody* love.

These qualities — love, compassion, peace — are not thoughts.

They are not ideas.

They are felt truths.

They arise only when we access a deeper part of our being — what we simply call the **heart**.

Why We Call It the Heart

To avoid unnecessary debates, philosophical arguments, or confusion from cultural terminology, we use one simple word: **heart**.

Not the physical heart, of course.

Not the organ that pumps blood.

But the *spiritual heart* — the center of awareness, presence, and deep connection. The place within you that doesn't think love, but *is* love. The part of you that doesn't analyze peace, but *rests* in it.

This spiritual heart doesn't belong to any religion.

It isn't tied to dogma or belief.

It is universal — as available to a child as it is to a sage.

And it can only be accessed when we go beyond the mind.

In Simplicity, We Find Truth

So in this book, and in our sharing, we keep it simple.

We call this center the **heart**.

Because that's what it feels like — the most intimate, open, and sincere part of ourselves.

It's where healing begins.

It's where love arises.

It's where peace is no longer a concept, but a living presence.

No more arguing about terms.

No more defending doctrines.

Just a gentle reminder: **return to the heart**.

Everything else will follow.

Chapter Twenty-Eight

Start Where You Can Feel - Your Body

We are a three-part being: **body**, **mind**, and **spirit** — or if you prefer, **the physical**, **the mental**, and **the energetic**. Each element influences the others. The mind shapes emotions, the heart influences vitality, and the body feeds back signals of comfort or distress to both. They are interconnected in ways more intimate than most books on happiness or spirituality acknowledge.

Many books and teachings emphasize cultivating the **mind**: meditation, mindfulness, positive thinking, letting go, reframing thoughts, and so on. These are powerful, yes. But have you noticed that very few talk about how to **nurture the heart**, or **invigorate the body**?

The truth is: **your heart and spirit can't flourish if your body is tired, weak, or stagnant.**

"A high-spirited body brings with it a joyful heart and a satisfying mind."

This is why we start with the **body**. Because it is **the most manageable** of the three.

You can't grab your mind with your hands. You can't poke at your spirit and say, "Here, fix this." But your body? You can move it. Breathe into it. Feel it. Strengthen it. Energize it.

And here's the beauty: **when you begin to energize your body, everything else follows.**

The **heart** starts to open. You begin to feel happy again, satisfied again. That childlike zest starts returning—not just emotionally, but hormonally. Your dopamine, oxytocin, and endorphins awaken. You smile more, and not because you "should," but because your cells are humming with life.

And then, something magical happens—**your mind quiets down**. You start worrying less. Not because you reasoned your way out of anxiety, but because **you feel too good to worry**.

"A contented heart is not the result of a calm mind, but the outcome of a body and spirit fully charged with energy."

In this book, we propose a simple shift: **stop over-working your mind**, and **start enlivening your body**. Here's why:

- The body is the **entry point**. It grounds you in the here and now.

- It gives you **instant feedback** — move it, and it responds.

- It's the most **neglected doorway to spiritual and emotional freedom**.

If you want sustained contentment, not just fleeting moments of joy, this is the foundation: **work on all three parts — body, mind, and spirit — but start where you can feel the results immediately: your body**.

So our journey begins here — not with philosophy or abstraction — but with the one thing you've always had, and perhaps overlooked: **your living, breathing, sensing, feeling, healing body**.

"Happiness is not something you think into being. It's something you feel, live, and move into existence."

Physical core of health

The **physical core of health** can be defined as the foundational center of our body's vitality, stability, and energy. It's not just about abs or muscles—it's the **deep integration of bodily systems** that support life and well-being. A good definition would include:

1. Structural Core (Anatomical)

- The muscles, bones, and connective tissues in the abdomen, lower back, pelvis, and hips.

- This structural core stabilizes movement, supports posture, and protects vital organs.

2. Energetic Core (TCM or Vitality Perspective)

- In Traditional Chinese Medicine, the core includes the **Dantian** (energy center below the navel), which is the reservoir of Qi (life force).

- It's the source of both physical stamina and internal vitality.

3. Functional Core (Organ Systems)

- Digestive, cardiovascular, and nervous systems centered in the torso.

- These systems must function harmoniously to supply nutrients, circulate energy, and manage stress.

4. Cellular Core (Biological)

- At the deepest level, our physical health is rooted in **cellular energy production** (mitochondrial health), nutrient absorption, and detoxification.

Summary:

The physical core of health is the central zone of life force, combining structural strength, organ vitality, and energy circulation. When this core is strong and clear, the whole body functions with ease, resilience, and harmony.

Core Health is Cellular Health

If there's one truth about healing the body that's often overlooked, it's this:

The core of all health begins at the cellular level.

We are made up of trillions of cells. Every function — thinking, walking, digesting, even healing — depends on whether our cells are energized and functioning well. And at the heart of each cell's energy system is something called the **mitochondria** — your body's natural power generator.

When your **mitochondria** are activated and healthy, they produce the energy (ATP) needed to repair tissues, fight off illness, restore balance, and rejuvenate your whole being. On the flip side, when they're weak or underperforming, disease and fatigue follow.

So the real secret to wellness?

Revitalize every cell. Heal everything.

How to Activate Mitochondria: Do This One Simple Thing

You don't need a pill or machine to boost your mitochondria.

You need **oxygen, blood flow**, and gentle **cellular motion**.

The best way?

Jog in place — slowly and rhythmically — for 30 minutes.

Do it **without panting**.

Panting is a sign that your body is running out of oxygen, which defeats the purpose. Mitochondria thrive in an **oxygen-rich environment**, so the goal is **slow, continuous movement** that keeps your blood flowing and your breath smooth.

This slow, stationary jogging:

- **Delivers oxygen** to every cell

- **Stimulates circulation**

- **Wakes up mitochondria**

- And **recharges your entire system** — gently, deeply, and safely

Every Cell Benefits

No matter where your health challenge lies — your brain, heart, joints, or hormones — once your cells begin to breathe and energize again, **healing begins** from the inside out.

This is the missing piece in modern health: Not treating the symptoms, but recharging the cells.

Chapter Twenty-Nine

Experience Your Inner Qi

I nward focusing forms the foundation of this transformative energizing practice. As we explore the profound benefits of directing our awareness inward, this chapter reveals how this ancient technique can unlock remarkable shifts in our energy, awareness, and overall well-being.

Inward focusing is the art of turning your attention fully inward — away from the noise of the outside world, away from the endless chatter of the mind — and anchoring it deeply within your own body's sensations and energy flow.

Many traditions teach this skill in different forms, but the essence is universal: when you quiet your outward senses and direct your awareness inward, you tap into a world of subtle power, movement, and vitality that is always there, waiting to be felt.

In my meditation classes, we often explore this through the lens of **qi flow** — the life energy that courses through our bodies, following the pathways known as **meridians** and gathering at vital energy centers, the **chakras**. We teach that to activate and guide this qi, you must first learn to *sense* it.

Let me guide you through one simple, yet powerful, exercise we use as a first lesson.

Exercise: Feeling the Qi Between Your Hands

1. **Prepare Your Posture**

- Sit comfortably — it doesn't matter if you're cross-legged on a cushion, seated on a chair, or even standing still. What matters is that your body is relaxed yet stable.

1. **Enter Prayer Position**

- Bring your hands together in front of your chest, palms pressed lightly against each other, in a simple prayer position. Close your eyes gently, let your shoulders drop, and take a few calm, natural breaths.

1. **Focus on the Center of Your Palms**

* Now, for the next three minutes, place your full awareness on the very center of your palms. Not thinking about them, not analyzing — just *feeling*. Feel into the tiny sensations, the warmth, the subtle pressure, or a slight tingling or pulsing. Be patient until you feel something in the middle of your palms.

1. **Separate the Hands and Begin Circular Motion**

* After three minutes, gently separate your hands by about three inches. Keep your left hand still, palm facing the right palm. With your right hand, begin making small circular movements, keeping it facing the left palm, as if you're stirring the air between them in a circle about three to four inches wide.

1. **Feel the Sensation Transfer**

- As you continue, you may begin to notice something remarkable: a subtle circular sensation rotating in your *left* palm, even though your left hand is not moving. It's as if the right hand's movement is creating a connection through the space, and your left hand is quietly receiving it.

1. **Increase the Distance**

- Once you feel this clearly, you can gradually increase the distance between your hands — first to a foot, then two, even three feet apart. If your inward focus is strong enough, you will still sense the circular motion from the right hand reaching across the empty space into the left.

Extending the Practice: Feeling the Navel Chakra

If you have been successful in feeling the circular movement of your left palm, let me introduce another practice.

Lie flat, face downward, either on a bed or a carpet. Form a fist with your left or right hand. Place it gently right on your belly button. Simply rest there for three minutes.

In about three or four minutes, you may begin to feel the vibration or pulsation at your belly button. That is where the **navel chakra** resides — a vital center of stored energy. This experience demonstrates the true power of inward focusing. Because you bring your attention to that area, the qi naturally concentrates there, making the vibration more detectable and alive to your senses.

It's important to note that while this technique is often used in **sitting meditation** (or **sitting Zen**), Since this particular book is *not* focused on sitting Zen practices. We have introduced the book of sitting meditation of our lineage in the Appendix 4 for those who wish to explore it further.

Instead, this book is focused on **motion Zen**, which we will explore in the next few chapters — practices that bring this same depth of inward focus into the flow and movement of daily life. Stay tuned as we step into the moving world of Zen-in-action.

Inward focusing unlocks a hidden world inside you — a world where thought becomes still, where sensation becomes vivid, and where your own hands can awaken the sleeping energy that has always been there.

Try on other parts of your body. Feel it. Let yourself be surprised by the quiet power that lives within you.

Chapter Thirty

Three-Center Alignment

A Meridian-Based Meditation for Qi Activation and Integration

This meditation method is designed to align and activate the three major energy centers—**the root (Earth), the heart (Human), and the crown (Heaven)**—to facilitate optimal qi (life force) flow throughout the body. It is a foundational practice for whole-body integration, spiritual awakening, and healing. Structural integrity is essential, so the posture must support a **straight spine** to allow smooth meridian flow.

Posture Setup: Foundation for Energy Alignment

- **Seated Position:** Sit on the floor in **at least a half-lotus position** (one foot on the opposite thigh). Full lotus is ideal but not necessary. You may use a cushion to elevate the hips and relieve pressure on your lower back, or knees.

- **Spine:** Keep your **spine straight**—this is non-negotiable. Your head should be balanced over your pelvis.

- **Chin:** Slightly **tuck your chin in** to lengthen the back of your neck and bring your head into alignment with your spine.

- **Hands:** Rest your hands **comfortably** on your thighs or knees, palms up or down—whichever feels more natural and grounded for you.

- **Eyes: Gently close your eyes** to turn your attention inward.

- **Heart:** Open your heart to be in charge.

- **Tongue: Curl your tongue** gently upward to touch the **roof of your mouth** (the soft palate), completing the microcosmic orbit.

Most important of all: Focus. You begin by focusing on the **path of your breathing**. Feel the qi as it enters through your nose, moves down your throat, and fills your lungs. Only through focus can you **redirect mental noise into the rhythm of your breathing**. This focus allows the wandering mind to settle and gradually become quiet.

Breathing Practice: Activating the Inner Current

Breathing is not just mechanical—it is energetic. Follow these **four golden rules**, known in Chinese as **(tiny), (long), (continuous), (gentle)**:

1. **Continuous**

   ○ Inhale and exhale as if drawing silk from a cocoon—**unbroken, seamless, and flowing**.

2. **Long**

   ○ Begin with a rhythm of **6 seconds in, 6 sec-**

onds out.

○ Over time, lengthen to **10 seconds in, 10 seconds out**.

3. **Tiny**

○ Use only a **thin stream of air**—quiet and subtle.

4. **Gentle**

○ Breathe with **softness and ease**. There should be no force, only natural continuity.

□ *Continue this breathing for several minutes while maintaining posture. Let your awareness begin to settle inward.*

Stage 1: Awakening the Navel Center

• **After five minutes, focus your awareness** approximately **three inches behind the belly button**—this is your **Navel Chakra** (also referred to as the Dantian in Taoist practice).

- This is the **core center** where prenatal qi from your mother nourished your body in the womb.

- It serves as the **gateway** to the meridian system.

□ Shift in Focus

Once you begin to feel the **flow of qi** or the **vibration of the chakra**, transfer your focus from the **path of your breathing** into the **specific area where you sense qi**. Whether it feels like tingling, pulsing, or warmth, let your attention rest there.

Remember: **Focus is the key to quieting the mind.** By concentrating on the qi sensations, the mind naturally releases wandering thoughts and becomes anchored in stillness.

□ Let the Qi Flow

As you continue to breathe and concentrate, you may feel a **wave of qi** radiating from your navel and flowing in the following pattern:

1. **Upward into the chest**

2. **Across the shoulders**

3. **Down the arms into the palms**

4. **Around the sides to the back**, especially the kidneys

5. **Down through the hips, legs, feet, and toes**

This is the **first stage** of Three-Center Alignment: **Whole-body qi activation**.

Stage 2: Root Chakra Expansion

Once you feel your body filled with qi, **shift your focus** to the **Root Chakra**:

- **For men**: the area near the **prostate**

- **For women**: the area near the **cervix**

□ What to Do

- Focus your attention on the **vibration** or **pulsing** sensation at the root.

- Allow it to **grow**:

  ○ From the size of a **golf ball**

  ○ To a **baseball**

  ○ Eventually to a **melon**, filling the **lower ab-domen**

As it expands, it will begin to **merge upward** into the **Heart Chakra**.

Stage 3: Heart Chakra Connection

- The **Heart Chakra** is located in the **center of your chest**.

- When you sense a **pulsation** or warmth here, **alternate your focus**:

  ○ Move awareness **between the Root and the Heart**.

  ○ You may start to notice a **channel** connecting them.

This connection is the beginning of what Taoist energy medicine calls the **Fire Channel**

Stage 4: Crown Chakra Alignment

- Next, shift your focus upward to the **Crown Chakra**, at the **top of your head**.

- When you begin to feel a **gentle pulsation** there, bring your attention to the **alignment** of all three centers:

1. **Root (Earth)**

2. **Heart (Human)**

3. **Crown (Heaven)**

You may have to **readjust your posture**:
- Sit **taller**

- **Tuck the chin** slightly more

- Feel the **vertical axis** of energy like a **column of light** going through your center.

Final Integration: Enter the Column of Light

- Once the **three centers are aligned**, and you feel a continuous flow of qi along this **central vertical axis,** maintain your focus.

- You may **see or sense** a **column of light** traveling through you.

- **Enter this column**.

This column represents your **connection to the universe**—a direct line between **Heaven (Crown), Human (Heart)**, and **Earth (Root)**.

Why Three-Center Alignment Matters

- The **Crown Chakra** represents center of **Heaven** .

- The **Root Chakra** represents center of **Earth**.

- The **Heart Chakra** is the center of **Human**.

When all three are aligned and connected, you are **harmonizing with the Dao**—balancing the cosmic forces of nature within your own body. This is the true meaning of **"Three-Center Alignment"** — center of **Heaven, Earth, and Humanity in One Body**.

Part IV

Each Moment is for Each of Us

Chapter Thirty-Two

Landing at The Other Shore

> **When you truly and wholeheartedly comprehend every perspective on the same subject, you no longer hold onto your own perspective.**

The Other Shore — Where is it?

Now that your body is energized and your awareness sharpened—with greater sensitivity and deeper objectivity—you begin to expand your consciousness beyond the confines of your personal view. You do this not by reinforcing your opinion, but by making a sincere effort to understand differing perspectives on the same subject.

At first, it may seem that others are simply mistaken or uninformed. But the more perspectives you explore, the more you begin to realize: the differences arise not from right or wrong, but from differing vantage points—different positions, life experiences, and levels of understanding. Every viewpoint is shaped by limited and often incomplete knowledge of the broader web of cause and effect.

When this truth settles in your heart, something beautiful happens. You begin to *accept* and *comprehend* every perspective, not out of politeness or passivity, but from a genuine understanding of their context. You see that each perspective holds a piece of the puzzle—not the whole truth, but a fragment of it.

And then—at that very moment—you transcend the need to defend your own perspective. You see through the illusion of ownership over thoughts and opinions. You recognize that your own point of view, born from a narrow sliver of experience, offers no more ultimate truth than any other.

When you can fully and honestly embrace all perspectives without clinging to one as your own, you step beyond the boundaries of the egoic mind. You enter a new dimension of awareness.

This is the moment you begin to awaken to **Universal Awareness**—a space where truth is no longer something to be claimed, but something to be witnessed in its wholeness. In this space, your consciousness is no longer confined by identity or ideology. It is open, inclusive, and expansive—just like the universe itself.

This is the beginning of what I call the **universal perspective**.

You become like the sky—capable of holding every kind of weather without being disturbed. Joy and sorrow, praise and blame, logic and emotion—they all pass through. But the sky remains. This is clarity without rigidity. Compassion without logic.

Where Is the Other Shore?

One of my fellow teachers once posed a deceptively simple question:

Where can I find "the other shore"?

In Buddhism, the "other shore" is a nickname for "Buddha Land", or "Heaven".

Many interpret it as a mystical destination—nirvana, enlightenment, or some faraway heaven. But he offered a more grounded and penetrating view. "The other shore," he said, "is the shore beyond your comfort zone. It is beyond the reasoning you've always agreed with. Beyond the beliefs that have kept you safe. Beyond the logic that made sense only to the old version of you."

In that moment, I understood:

The other shore is not somewhere else—it is somewhere wider, much wider.

It is the unfamiliar territory that exists just beyond the edge of your habitual thinking, your cherished narratives, and your need for security.

Crossing the River of Identity

To reach the other shore is to take that step, to cross that river. Not with effort or ambition, but with humility. You don't need to push. You only need to loosen your grip—on what you think you know, on who you think you are, on what you think truth should be.

And here's the paradox:

By the time you agree with all perspectives,

by the time you accept them all wholeheartedly,

you have already crossed the river.

You have stepped into a space where all shores are welcomed, even contradictory ones. And in doing so, you have surrendered—not as defeat, but as acceptance.

You have harmonized yourself to the universe. Or to God. Or to Buddha. Or to nature.

At that point, **labels no longer matter.**

Words like "God," "spirit," "truth," or "awareness" are like fingers pointing to the moon—they helped you start the journey, but now, you no longer stare at the finger. You are bathing in moonlight.

The Moment of Acceptance

When you arrive at this shoreless state, you don't need to protect your viewpoint anymore. You don't need to resist others. You don't even need to convince yourself. The old divisions begin to fade:

you versus me,

right versus wrong,

this belief versus that belief.

You begin to breathe with the universe.

You begin to see with its eyes.

This is not a philosophical conclusion.

It is a lived state.

You don't arrive by force, but by letting go.

That is what it means to expand consciousness.

That is what it means to awaken.

All Shores Are One

It is not a matter of arrival, but of acceptance.

Not about defining, but about embodying.

Not about seeking another shore, but about realizing—

You were never apart from it to begin with.

All shores, once seen as separate, dissolve into one.

And you, no longer a traveler or a seeker, simply remain—

open, aware, at peace with everything as it is.

Chapter Thirty-Three

Seeing Beyond the Waves

We Are All Like Waves in the Ocean

I n my view—and perhaps I could say it this way—we are not separate from each other. We are like waves in the vast ocean, each rising and falling, shaped by the waves beside us, behind us, and before us. And those neighboring waves are not fixed either; each of them is also affected by the waves around them, layer by layer, like an infinite web of motion and influence. Our form, our thoughts, our reactions—they ripple outward and inward, just like every other wave around us. No wave stands alone in isolation.

Forces Beyond the Surface

But the story doesn't end there. There is also wind—forces we cannot see but surely feel—blowing across the surface of our lives. There are deep undercurrents as well, subtle but powerful, shaping us from beneath. These invisible influences—our inherited patterns, the unspoken emotions of those around us, ancestral energy, social conditioning—are all part of the same oceanic dance.

Karma: The Unavoidable Flow

This interplay of causes and conditions is what we often call karma. But karma is not a punishment or a scorecard. It is simply **cause and effect**, the law of nature. It moves without bias, without need for improvement, and beyond human control. It cannot be escaped, outsmarted, or manipulated. Like gravity, it just *is*.

So what can we do?

We can face it. Face it with courage. Face it with love. That, in my experience, is the only way to relate to karma skillfully.

The Wisdom of Distance:

(Li Xiang)

The teaching I received on how to live with karma comes from the Chinese concept of (*Li Xiang*), which means "to distance from form." It doesn't mean to ignore form, to deny it, to forget it, or to reject it. It means to take a step back. To **be with** the phenomenon—be it a person, an object, a thought, or a situation—without being entangled by it.

By practicing *Li Xiang*, we learn to keep a healthy distance from form—not as a means of escape, but as a way of expanding our vision. When we are no longer stuck inside the form, we begin to see more of what is going on. We notice the chain of causes and conditions behind it. We begin to understand not just the surface-level interaction, but the larger movement—what gave rise to it, what it's connected to, and what it's likely to lead to.

Rising Above the Waves

This is the expansion of awareness.

If we remain as a single wave on the surface, we can only see what is immediately around us—those waves we crash into, the ones just ahead, or behind. At this level, our vision is blocked. We cannot see what is influencing our neighbors because their view is obstructed by other waves—just like ours is.

But what if we rise above the waves?

If we can elevate ourselves, even just a little—rise above the surface, become the sky watching the sea—we begin to see with a wider perspective. Suddenly, it's not just *our* wave we see. We see the neighboring waves, and the waves surrounding those, and even the wider, subtler motions that have been shaping them from afar. We see layers upon layers of waves—ripples of cause and effect, moving through the whole ocean.

When we rise above, we begin to understand. We begin to *see*.

The Bond of Karma: Clarity with Compassion

And when we truly see—when we see clearly how each wave is affected by countless other waves—we realize something profound:

No one escapes this ocean.

Not a single person is free from the tangle of interconnected motion. Everyone is tightly bound by the waves of cause and effect—some from lifetimes ago, some only moments old. And in that realization, something unexpected may arise within us: not despair, but a deep sense of sadness, a kind of helpless knowing.

You recognize the immense complexity of karma. You realize how little control anyone has, how difficult it is to escape habitual patterns, generational pain, societal conditioning, and emotional reactions.

And then—without trying—compassion arises.

Not as an ideal. Not as a practice. But as a natural response to the truth of our shared entanglement. Once you see clearly, you cannot help but feel for others. You begin to accept their struggles gently, without judgment.

This is **clarity with compassion**. It is not cold detachment. It is not naïve optimism. It is love that sees things as they are and still chooses to stay open.

The practice of distancing from form gives us this clarity. It helps us live in harmony with karma—not by trying to outrun it, but by understanding its dance, feeling its depth, and showing up with presence and care.

When compassion rises, wisdom will arrive with answers.

Chapter Thirty-Four

Relax and Let It Flow

"The moment you stop trying to shine, you begin to glow."

— Anonymous

In today's world, we're often taught that success comes from pressure and force. Push harder. Do more. Yet the most extraordinary moments in life—those of clarity, precision, and brilliance—tend to happen when we are not trying hard at all.

Science calls this the *flow state*, but I knew it long before I knew the term. It's a state where the mind lets go, and life begins to move through you.

The Composition That Wrote Itself

It was 1955. I was ten years old, in fifth grade, in Shanghai. That day, our teacher, Miss Lu Hezhen, gave us a writing assignment: *On the Bus Stop.*

I picked up my pencil, and before I knew it, the story was pouring out. I didn't pause. I didn't plan. I didn't even use an eraser. Within fifteen minutes, it was finished.

To me, it was nothing special. But to Miss Lu, it was. She gave me 101 points out of 100. That moment stayed with me—not because I felt smart, but because I realized something could come *through* me, without effort. That was my first taste of flow.

Coding Without Time

Years later, in my career as a software developer, I'd revisit that same state.

Some tasks took days of methodical effort—but then there were those moments when everything clicked. I'd sit down, and within two hours, finish what would normally take four struggling days. No bugs. No mistakes. Just fluid creation, one line of code after another.

In those moments, time vanished. So did self-doubt. I wasn't thinking—I was *doing*. And yet, it didn't feel like I was doing at all. It was as if the program was writing itself through me.

Becoming Qi

In my later years, my journey turned inward—toward meditation, Qi Gong, and the subtle energy systems of the body.

Often, during deep meditation, I felt Qi flooding through me so completely that my body disappeared. There were no limbs, no muscles, no skin—just pulsing, flowing energy. It was serene. Expansive. I wasn't meditating. I was floating like a cloud.

Again and again, that familiar feeling returned: effortless, timeless, joyful. It was flow—not of words or logic, but of pure being.

Flow on the Fairway

Even in the most physical of tasks, flow can take over.

I was once a handicap 8 golfer. I practiced often, played regularly. But there was one game where everything changed. That day, I shot a 73—far beyond my usual performance.

What stood out was that I didn't swing hard. I wasn't forcing anything. My movements felt natural, even lazy. But the ball flew straighter, landed better. Everything just... worked. To this day, I still don't know how I did it. I didn't *try* harder. I actually tried *less*—and that made all the difference.

Kobe in the Zone

Even elite athletes know this zone. Take Kobe Bryant—he once scored 81 points in a single NBA game. Think about that. Every shot, every movement, had to be precise, fluid, unbroken. If he had paused for just one second—if he had *thought* too much or hesitated—he would have missed.

That kind of performance isn't born from trying harder. It's born from being in complete harmony with the moment.

That's flow.

The Truth About Flow

Here's what I've come to understand:

Flow is not a reward for effort.

It is the *absence* of effort.

The more we try to grasp it, the more it slips away. But the moment we release, it arrives—naturally. Flow lives in the rhythm of the breath, the stillness behind action, the joy that arises when the self steps aside.

Watch a child at play. Watch a dancer lost in movement. Or a craftsman so immersed in their work that hours feel like minutes. In these moments, there's no striving. Only doing. Only being.

A Gentle Invitation

If you've ever tasted that feeling—where effort vanishes and everything clicks—you've already met flow. And if you haven't, don't worry. You don't need to chase it. In fact, chasing is what prevents it.

Instead, return to simplicity. Do what you love with no thought of outcome. Let your breath guide you. Soften into the moment.

Flow will find you when you stop looking.

Let it come. And when it does—smile.

Chapter Thirty-Five

Unleash the Power of Love

The Intention That Shapes Reality

In the late 1990s, Japanese researcher **Dr. Masaru Emoto** conducted a simple yet astonishing experiment. He exposed water to different words, images, and music, then froze it and photographed the ice crystals.

What he found captivated the world:

Water that had been exposed to positive words like *"love"* or *"gratitude"* formed beautiful, symmetrical crystals—like tiny snowflakes from heaven. But water exposed to words like *"hate"* or *"you fool"* formed chaotic, distorted patterns, or no pattern at all.

It was as if water, the most basic element of life, could feel.

Or more accurately—it could *respond to intention*.

Critics questioned the scientific rigor, but the core message stuck:

Our thoughts and emotions carry energy. And that energy can shape the physical world.

Let me ask you another way.

If someone says to you, "I love you," can you feel whether it's genuine or not?

Can you sense their heart behind the words?

Doesn't that tell you something about the *power of intentions*?

The Fish Who Didn't Like Me

Years ago, I had an experience that drove this message deeper than any experiment ever could.

I was dining at a busy seafood restaurant in Hong Kong. I pointed to a fish swimming in the tank, asking the waiter to have it cooked for dinner. As the fish was pulled out, I was suddenly struck by a sharp, piercing headache. I paused, surprised. Was it just coincidence?

But then it happened again. And again.

Every time I selected a live creature for a meal, a sharp pain came over me.

I remember joking with myself, *"I guess what the fish is trying to tell me in the fish language is—he does not like me."*

Years later, I had a similar experience while dropping lobsters into a steamer. The pain returned—quick, sharp, and eerily familiar. It was as if a silent thread of connection had been torn.

That's when I began to understand something subtle, but life-changing:

We are not separate.

What we do—what we *intend*—is felt, even when no words are spoken. There is a shared field of life. The boundaries we believe in—between species, between minds, even between moments—are more porous than we think.

A Glimpse of One Mind

Perhaps this is what the great spiritual traditions mean when they speak of *one consciousness*. Not as a philosophical abstraction, but as a lived, felt reality. That underneath all forms, we are connected. That intention flows across invisible threads, weaving a single web of life.

And in that web, what you send out—love or fear, gratitude or judgment—*matters*. Not just for you, but for all of us.

Now, Imagine This...

Imagine you turn your heart toward love—not just in thought, but in intention.

Imagine directing that love toward your family.

Toward your colleagues.

Even toward people you struggle with.

What kind of world would begin to emerge?

What if love was not something we *feel* occasionally, but something we *broadcast*—as naturally as the sun gives light?

If your intention truly shapes the world around you, then what greater power could you possibly wield than the **intention of love**?

Unleash it. Let it ripple.

Let the universe sing in harmony—through you.

Chapter Thirty-Six

One Is All. All Is One

In the ancient Zen classic *Xin Xin Ming*, the Third Patriarch Sengcan wrote a simple yet profound line:

"One is all, all is one."

These words are not meant to be poetic or philosophical; they point directly to the nature of reality. Everything we see, hear, feel, and experience — every tree, cloud, emotion, star — emerges from a single source. And just as a wave is never separate from the ocean, nothing in this universe is separate from that source.

"The universe never makes a mistake." -Dr. John Young

It does not judge, it does not divide. It simply flows — in wholeness, in harmony. Our suffering arises only when we fragment this flow, when we carve out a separate identity and call it "me."

Detachment as Reconnection

In previous chapters, we explored detachment — not as rejection, but as a reorientation. Detachment is simply the act of **shifting our attention from the little ego to the vast universe**. The ego sees limitation, comparison, and control. The universe sees interconnectedness, acceptance, and rhythm. When we detach, we are not stepping away from life, but stepping **into** life — as it truly is.

This is what Zen refers to as the **beginner's mind** — the mind at the very beginning. Before conditioning, before opinions, before labels. It is **one mind**, pure and receptive, open and aware. It is not a mind that knows, but a mind that is present.

Echoes Across Traditions

This truth — that all arises from One — is echoed across spiritual traditions:

- In Christianity, Jesus said, **"I and the Father are one."(John 10:30).**

- This is not a claim of status but a statement of unity. The same spirit that breathed life into him breathes life into all of us.

- In Advaita Vedanta, **Sri Ramana Maharshi** taught that the true Self is not the body or mind, but **pure consciousness** — the same consciousness in all beings.

- *"There are not many selves. There is only One Self, and you are That."*

- In Zen, **Huang Po** said, *"All the Buddhas and all sentient beings are nothing but the One Mind."*

- What we call "you" and "me" are simply temporary ripples on the same lake.

These teachings all point to the same door:

We must shift from the egoic view to the universal view.

The Role of Qi — Your Spiritual Platform

But how do we make that shift?

It cannot be done by force. It cannot be done by thought. It is done by **energy**.

In Traditional Chinese Medicine, we speak of **Qi** — the vital life force that animates all things. Without Qi, awareness becomes dull. The mind dominates, the heart retreats. The ego thrives in this low-energy environment, filling the void with stories, fears, and judgments.

But when Qi is abundant — when it flows smoothly through your meridians and nourishes every cell — your awareness sharpens. You begin to **feel more**, **see more clearly**, and most importantly, because you physically feel energized, you begin to **let go**.

You begin to surrender.

Surrender as Acceptance

But let's be clear:

Surrender is not giving up.

Surrender is receiving.

To surrender to God — or the Universe, the Dao, the One — is to **accept everything that Life offers you**, with gratitude and openness. It is to trust the intelligence of the universe, the timing of events, the meaning of challenges.

When we accept all, we no longer resist anything.

When we resist nothing, there is no conflict.

When there is no conflict, there is no suffering.

This is not liberation from life, but **liberation into life**.

Now We Are Living in Heaven or Buddha Land

When we align with One Consciousness — when we accept all that life brings without resistance, when we no longer judge, fight, or divide — something profound happens:

We realize that we are already **home**.

We are not waiting to enter heaven.

We are not striving to reach Buddhaland.

We are living in it — right now.

Heaven is not a distant realm in the sky.

Buddhaland is not a myth or a metaphor.

They are names for a state of being where **everything is embraced**, and nothing is left out.

In this state, we no longer seek perfection — we see that everything is already perfect, just as it is.

We no longer chase freedom — we discover that **freedom arises naturally** when we stop resisting.

We no longer search for peace — we feel peace **because we are no longer at war with what is**.

In this moment of unity with the One, **we are as a child again** — present, trusting, playful, and whole.

We are not becoming someone special.

We are simply returning to our natural state in the now.

In every moment

Smile and enjoy the flow of life with your heart.

Practice the second layer of fulfillment.

Look beyond the waves.

Trust the universe

Unleash the power of loving intention.

Enjoy the flow.

Be The One.

Chapter Thirty-Eight

Appendix 1: Introduction to Zen Meditation

https://www.zencosmos.com.tw/product/□□□□/

https://www.zencosmos.com.tw/prod-uct/%E7%A6%AA%E5%9D%90%E5%85%A5%E9%96%80/

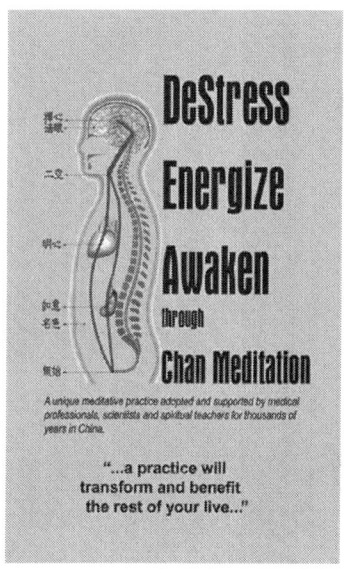

https://www.amazon.com/dp/1456466410

Printed in Dunstable, United Kingdom